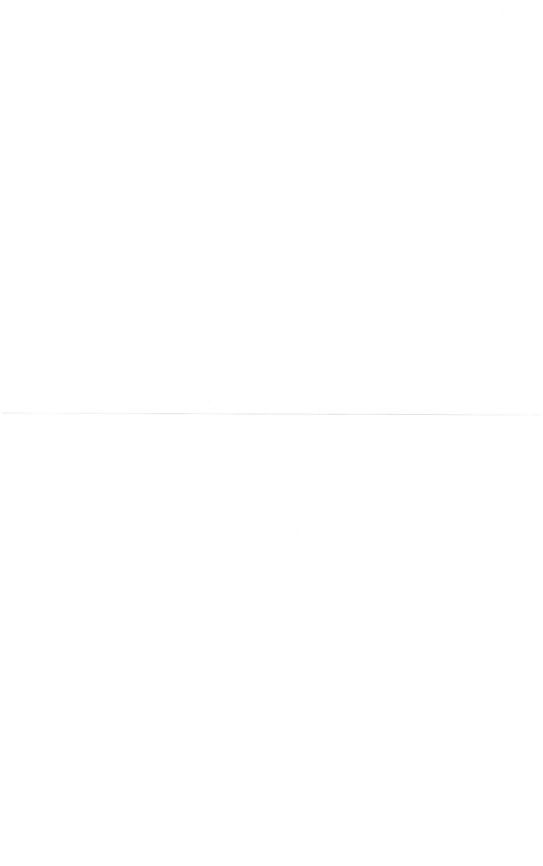

Isaura Barrera, Ph.D. & Lucinda Kramer, Ph.D.

SKILLED DIALOGUE

AUTHENTIC COMMUNICATION AND COLLABORATION ACROSS DIVERSE Perspectives

BALBOA
PRESS
A DIVISION OF HAY HOUSE

Balboa Press books may be ordered through booksellers or by contacting:

Balboa Press
A Division of Hay House
1663 Liberty Drive
Bloomington, IN 47403
www.balboapress.com
1 (877) 407-4847

Because of the dynamic nature of the Internet, any web addresses or links contained in this book may have changed since publication and may no longer be valid. The views expressed in this work are solely those of the author and do not necessarily reflect the views of the publisher, and the publisher hereby disclaims any responsibility for them.

The author of this book does not dispense medical advice or prescribe the use of any technique as a form of treatment for physical, emotional, or medical problems without the advice of a physician, either directly or indirectly. The intent of the author is only to offer information of a general nature to help you in your quest for emotional and spiritual well-being. In the event you use any of the information in this book for yourself, which is your constitutional right, the author and the publisher assume no responsibility for your actions.

Any people depicted in stock imagery provided by Thinkstock are models, and such images are being used for illustrative purposes only.
Certain stock imagery © Thinkstock.

Print information available on the last page.

ISBN: 978-1-5043-8545-9 (sc)
ISBN: 978-1-5043-8546-6 (e)

Library of Congress Control Number: 2017912222

Balboa Press rev. date: 08/29/2017

Contents

PART I:
DIFFERENCES

Introduction

Whether intriguing, frustrating, challenging or even threatening, the challenges that diversity can pose for communication and collaboration are difficult to ignore or deny. These challenges, however, need not be negative ones. They can in fact offer incredible opportunities for positive communication and collaboration.

Growing up on the Texas-Mexico border I (Barrera) learned this aspect of diversity's challenges at an early age. By the age of six I needed to learn a new language and a new set of behaviors for success at school while retaining the language and behaviors I knew for negotiating life in my home border community. I saw the consequences when this challenge was perceived negatively as one that presented the choice of one language and set of behaviors at the expense of the other. It did not take long for me to realize that perceiving differences in this either-or fashion, neither minding them properly nor mining them appropriately, resulted in separation and division rather than inclusion and unity. It has since become increasingly clear that placing differences in separate and contradictory categories severely limits both communication and collaboration.

The premise of Skilled Dialogue, the topic of this text, is a straightforward one: that to communicate and collaborate optimally across diverse perspectives it is necessary to tap into the "power of the other" (Cloud, 2016); i.e., what the other brings to the interaction, as well as into the power of paradox; i.e., how differences can be additive rather than subtractive. In general, the power of the other tends to remain largely unacknowledged or to be acknowledged only negatively.

The power of paradox similarly remains largely untapped. Yet, when both of these powers are tapped, collaboration and communication can occur even in situations where they are believed to be impossible.

Significant disruptions in our ability to communicate and collaborate meaningfully with those who think, act or believe differently from us are being increasingly evidenced today. They are occurring not only on a global scale between countries and cultures, they are also becoming increasingly apparent on the smaller scale of everyday personal and professional interactions.

Apparently, it is not only becoming more challenging to communicate and collaborate across different perspectives, it is also becoming difficult to even hear different perspectives. In a 3/10/14 blog posting, Greg Lukianoff, president and CEO of the Foundation for Individual Rights in Education, made the following striking observation regarding a university's "disinvitation" of commencement speakers because of their views on particular issues: "freedom of speech and academic freedom depend on our ability to handle hearing opinions we dislike and constructively and creatively engaging with those opinions."[1] This ability to handle hearing differing opinions is critical. It is needed far beyond the freedom of speech and academic freedom. It is needed for our own welfare, the welfare of others, and of the earth itself. Without it, diversity of perspectives will continue to separate and divide us, impoverishing the communication and collaboration necessary to protect and promote that welfare.

Our own experiences as developers and trainers of Skilled Dialogue reflect this growing disruption in people's abilities to communicate meaningfully and craft productive collaborations with those who think, act or believe differently. Participants who came to our early workshops and professional development sessions on Skilled Dialogue to learn about using Skilled Dialogue with culturally diverse families and co-workers almost always ended up asking how they could apply it to situations with families, friends, neighbors and co-workers. The latter were not at all culturally diverse yet our workshop participants still experienced significant difficulty communicating and collaborating with them because of their diverse opinions, behaviors and values.

Skilled Dialogue is a proactive tool for converting diversity from challenge to opportunity; i.e., for mining and minding its riches. It is a field-tested approach designed to tap into and leverage the power of the other and the power of paradox. Through Skilled Dialogue interactions with diverse others can be crafted in ways that allow differences to enrich rather than limit available options and opportunities (Barrera, I., Corso, R., & Macpherson, D., 2003; Barrera, I., Kramer, L., & Macpherson, D., 2012; Barrera, I. & Kramer, L., 2009).

Overview of Content

Part I of this text (Chapters 1-3) sets the context for Skilled Dialogue by providing foundational information on three topics: diversity, paradox, and dialogue. Chapter 1 addresses diversity as a relational and comparative reality that exists *between* individuals rather than as a static reality within individuals' identities (e.g., cultural, gender, sexual orientation). Two aspects of diversity understood in this wider sense are discussed: the type of differences involved and the type of responses to those differences.

Chapter 2 extends the discussion of diversity by introducing the concept of paradox, the phenomenon of two or more apparently contradictory realities being simultaneously true. Ellinor and Gerard (2014, Kindle Loc. 1503) posed the question "As the world speeds up and the [multiplicity of diverse perspectives] becomes more and more obvious, how [can] we hold multiple viewpoints and still move ahead with aligned action?" Skilled Dialogue actively seeks to create an interactional space within which multiple viewpoints can be aligned so as to promote optimum communication and collaboration. Learning to think paradoxically is essential to the creation of such space because, without paradoxical thinking, diversity's contrasts all too easily deteriorate into a "one right answer" frame of mind able to create only either-or contradictions that privilege one view over another. When perceived through the lens of paradox, however, these same contradictions can be understood as mutually complementary contrasts, without need for forced choice between them. They can then be given equal voice and, consequently, mined for their riches in a collaborative context.

Part I culminates with Chapter 3. In this chapter, the authors first discuss the purpose and form of dialogue as a process grounded in a particular understanding of both diversity and paradox. They identify the characteristics of dialogue and contrast them with those associated with other interactional approaches. Skilled Dialogue is then addressed more specifically as each of its primary elements is discussed: qualities, dispositions and strategies. This discussion lays the groundwork for the more detailed discussion of these elements in Part II.

Part II (Chapters 4-7) focuses specifically on the Skilled Dialogue elements, starting with a description of its dispositions in Chapter 4. It first addresses how the first disposition, Choosing Relationship over Control, capitalizes on tapping into the "power of the other" (Cloud, 2016) by intentionally connecting individuals' perspectives in ways that (a) honor identities and voices no matter how diverse, (b) establish reciprocity so that those identities and voices can be expressed, and (c) promote responsiveness. Setting the Stage for Miracles, Skilled Dialogue's second and complementary disposition, is then addressed. This disposition capitalizes on the power of paradox and the interconnectedness of knowledge (Anderson, 2016). It involves the willingness to suspend preset agendas in order to better listen for what may lie beyond current understandings; i.e., for "what is waiting to emerge" (Jaworski, 1996, p. 182).

Together, these two dispositions support the successful implementation of Skilled Dialogue's six intertwined strategies, which are addressed in Chapters 5-7. (Note: Though discussed in a sequential and linear sequence in these chapters, the strategies are neither in reality. Examples of the interdependence and nonlinearity of the strategies in action are provided in Part III.)

Chapter 5 focuses on Skilled Dialogue's first two strategies: *Welcoming* and *Allowing*. These focus on honoring identity by focusing on affirming and respecting individuals' identities, however inappropriate or "wrong" we might perceive or judge them to be, while simultaneously affirming and respecting our own identity.

More specifically, *Welcoming*'s purpose is to communicate that we look forward to talking with and learning from those with whom we interact. It involves authentically communicating that interaction with another is welcomed as more than just a task to be accomplished.

Allowing complements *Welcoming*. It addresses allowing time for the other to express his/her perspective without interruption or discussion. Its purpose is to communicate our acknowledgment that the other's voice is valid; i.e., worthy of being expressed.

Sense-making and *Appreciating*, addressed in Chapter 6, are strategies that typically follow *Welcoming* and *Allowing*. Their purpose is to establish a context of reciprocity. Both strategies aim to recognize and affirm the potential contributions diverse perspectives can bring to an interaction. *Sense-making* accomplishes this by focusing on how an individual's diverse perspectives are evidence-based and not merely the result of "not knowing better," or "not knowing the right way," as they are so often unfortunately interpreted. It is a strategy used in seeking to learn how diverse perspectives are valid; i.e., of value within particular contexts. *Appreciating* is the corollary strategy that then is used to communicate appreciation of those diverse beliefs/behaviors as valued and valuable within the contexts in which they were acquired, though they may admittedly be of little value or even counterproductive outside those contexts. Skilled Dialogue's subsequent strategies, *Joining* and *Harmonizing,* become possible only when we can make sense of another's diverse beliefs and behaviors and appreciate their value for that other and often even for ourselves.

Chapter 7 addresses these last strategies, *Joining* and *Harmonizing*. These are designed to establish and communicate responsiveness to another rather than merely response or reactivity. Responsiveness is a quality that must be grounded in both respect and reciprocity to be authentic. Unfortunately it is also often a quality not fully understood. At its core, responsiveness recognizes that interactions across differences are about more than finding answers or being compassionate. Rather, they are about creating an interactional space within which the whole can be more than the sum of individual perspectives; that is, responsiveness creates a space within which two perspectives or choices (e.g., your way, my way; A, B; blue, yellow) are integrated to yield a third that is inclusive of both (e.g., our way; A + B = C; blue + yellow = green).

The strategies of *Joining* and *Harmonizing* leverage the power of paradox. They focus on generating a 3rd *Space* within which contradictions become complementary and can be integrated to yield a greater whole. (Note: The concept of 3rd Space is introduced in Chapter 2.) *Joining* first aims to get to a point where a listener can represent—though not necessarily agree with—another's diverse view to such a degree that the other feels heard and validated. Through communicating that other's diverse perspective, belief, value or behavior is truly understood, *Joining* builds the mutual engagement necessary for subsequent harmonizing of diverse perspectives. *Harmonizing* focuses on identifying a common substratum across differences that allows for their integration into inclusive realities without either concession or compromise. This strategy, which taps fully into the power of paradox, is perhaps the least familiar and most challenging of all the Skilled Dialogue strategies.

Though laid out in separate sections, the information in Chapters 1-7 is highly interrelated. Readers will find different aspects of it referred to implicitly and explicitly in sections other than those in which they are initially addressed. Nevertheless, we recommend that the book's chapters be read in sequence, at least initially, in order to facilitate the fullest understanding.

Part III, Chapters 8-11, focuses directly on the implementation of Skilled Dialogue. It translates the information in Parts I and II into concrete and practical action. Chapter 8 discusses paradox and 3rd Space, providing examples of what these look like in interactions between individuals holding diverse perspectives yet seeking to communicate and collaborate. Resources and activities that the authors have found useful in learning and teaching paradox and 3rd Space are also included. Chapter 9 revisits the Skilled Dialogue strategies, providing examples and non-examples of each in relation to specific interactions. Chapter 10 pulls all this information together. It first provides a brief summary of the Skilled Dialogue followed by a detailed description of its steps. A simulation activity is then provided, followed by several hypothetical cases for use in applying those steps to actual scenarios where diversity presents significant challenges to communication and collaboration. Finally, in Chapter 11 the authors provide a guide and self-assessment form for use in practicing and using Skilled Dialogue along with an interaction analysis form for reflecting on the presence or absence of Skilled Dialogue strategies in specific interactions.

Chapter 1

Diversity

"In embracing the diversity of human beings, we will find a surer way to be happy" (Gladwell, 2006)

It is so much easier to communicate and collaborate with people who agree with us or are at least willing to listen to our opinions and perspectives without argument or disagreement. Yet, we cannot simply exclude those who disagree with us from our lives. Often, they are family, friends, neighbors, colleagues, and people we supervise or who supervise us. At times, they may even be the same person, on our side on certain topics and strongly "against" us on others. At other times they may be individuals with whom we must work closely for short periods of time. As a non-tenured beginning faculty at a university there were often senior faculty who did not agree with me (Barrera) or see things as I did. I wanted to keep my job; at the same time I did not want to lose my voice. The tension between these two goals inspired the early development of Skilled Dialogue. I wondered if it was possible to honor my own views without disregarding others that seemed to contradict them.

Activity: Think for a moment. What words do you associate with differences of opinions or of viewpoints, beliefs, and behaviors?

Were most of your words negative or positive? Were words like "enriching" or "connecting" on your list of words? Why or why not?

Diversity of perspectives, opinions, beliefs or values all too often tends to be associated more with division and diminishment than with connection and enrichment. Yet, how we respond to diversity in any given interaction is more the function of how we understand it than of the presence of differences. Two aspects in particular are important to the understanding of diversity: what we believe to be its nature and what we believe are its roots or source. How we address these can determine whether our dialogue with others is skilled enough to enrich and connect us across our differences or not.

The nature of diversity

Diversity is commonly thought of as an objective attribute. In reality, however, diversity is a relational attribute. That is, it does not exist *within* a person (e.g., this or that person is diverse) but rather lives in the relational space *between* persons (e.g., that person is diverse *from me*).

People (or communities) can only be diverse *in reference to* a designated group or individual who is also of necessity diverse from them. A man, for example, would be considered diverse (in regard to his gender) in comparison to a woman or group of women. On the other hand, he would not be considered similarly diverse in comparison to another man or group of men. "In a galaxy, the space between two flickering stars … contains a gravitational pull that shapes their relationship" (Shapiro, 2017, p. 9). Anagolously, it is how people perceive and experience the differences between them that consequently shapes their relationship.

It is only in relationships that diversity's riches can be unleashed and harvested. Diversity is not about "that" person(s) independently of who is interacting with that person; it is and can only be about that person(s) in relation to another. *Naming another as diverse simultaneously also names as diverse those who are doing the naming.* That is, when I name an individual or group as diverse I am simultaneously also naming myself as diverse (from them). My own views and beliefs become diverse as I encounter views and beliefs different from my own. Diversity is, thus, never about who *they* are; it is about who *we* are.

Sources of diversity.

There are, of course, many sources of diversity, not all of which are of similar importance. Some are relatively unimportant, presenting little if any challenge to either communication or collaboration. What foods you eat or whether you believe strongly in set bedtimes for children, for example, makes little or no significant impact on communication or collaboration outside of specific contexts (e.g., if we're planning a joint dinner party or if as a teacher I believe set bedtimes are critical to children's abilities to concentrate).

Other differences, however, have a much stronger impact on communication and collaboration. These are differences that, typically, tend to be associated with social markers such as culture, ethnicity, religion, or lifestyle. These larger differences are typically assumed to be reliable markers of challenges to communication and collaboration. They are not, however, the reliable indicators of diversity's challenges that we believe them to be. While I may be from one culture and you from another we may, for example, have few other salient differences. We may speak the same language, have similar occupations, belong to the same church and participate in the same social activities. On the other hand, we may have the same cultural affiliation yet find significant interpersonal differences disrupting our communication and collaboration. I may, for example, adhere to the traditional values and practices of a culture while you may hold to that same cultural affiliation yet hold values and practices less in conformity with its traditional values and practices. Or, we may belong to different religions and hold very different values.

The authors have found that several sources of differences tend to be more reliable predictors of challenges to communication and collaboration than simple cultural affiliations and other similar external markers (Barrera, Corso, and Macpherson, 2003). They are, consequently, the sources that Skilled Dialogue addresses: funds of knowledge, sense of self, and perceptions and understandings of power.

Funds of knowledge. The first major source of diversity is differences in funds of knowledge; that is, in the knowledge a person brings to specific interactions, particularly that knowledge they believe factual. This knowledge may or may not be directly tied to culture, religion, gender or other such markers. When there are unacknowledged or unrecognized differences between people in the knowledge they believe essential to operate in and make sense of the world, the likelihood of miscommunication and failed collaboration is high regardless of differences in gender, cultural affiliation, religion, or other such categories.

All of us have built funds of knowledge composed of the information we have acquired about (a) the nature of the world around us (e.g., cooperative or not, containing abundant resources or only limited resources); (b) how it works (e.g., what signals opportunity and what does not); and (c) how it is best understood (e.g., what is acceptable and what is not, what signals respect and what does not). These funds of knowledge include information such as the following: information about social roles and rules, values and beliefs about how to best solve problems and make decisions, roles and rules for collaboration, the relative value of verbal and nonverbal communication. They can also include information specific to the content of a given interaction. Someone may, for example, *know* with absolute certainty that collaboration requires an identified leader while the person(s) with whom they seek to collaborate knows, with equal certainty, that leadership need not be assigned to a single person. When this is the case, the likelihood is high that they will have difficulty or at least high levels of frustration as they attempt to collaborate. Another example might be when one person assumes that what they know about the topic(s) addressed in an interaction is also known in the same way by the person(s) with whom they are interacting and, consequently, assumes there is no need for explanations or clarifications. When unrecognized or unacknowledged, these and other similar mismatches in funds of knowledge increase the likelihood of miscommunication and failed or limited collaboration.

Sense of self. A second source of diversity that commonly challenges communication and collaboration is differences in sense of self; that is, in "how you are, what you hold as important, and how you conceive of meaning in your life" (Shapiro, 2017, p. 9). Our sense of self defines who we are in relation to others and who others are in relation to us as well as how we each perceive the other in relation to ourselves.

Sense of self is a subset of funds of knowledge that is inclusive of principles and values, allegiances, meaningful customs and meaningful memories. It nevertheless deserves its own category because differences in sense of self tend to be less well-recognized or explicitly acknowledged in interactions than other funds of knowledge.

A person's sense of self includes whom they believe themselves to be as well as the status they believe is or should be accorded to that identity (e.g., how I believe others tend to, or should, perceive me, how much power I have or believe I have vis-à-vis those with those I am interacting). It also includes the behaviors associated with personal positive characteristics (e.g., goodness, competence) as well as those associated with negative characteristics (irresponsibility, incompetence). Values, ideals and convictions are also part of our sense of self as are meaningful experiences that have shaped those values, ideals and convictions.

The authors have found that individuals' sense of self can be the most challenging type of differences in regard to communication and collaboration. It is not entirely uncommon at times to sacrifice respectful communication and collaboration for the sake of maintaining a sense of self we wish respected. It can, for example, become more important to be perceived as competent than to communicate respect for another's opinions or views. [2]

If, for example, I have built my sense of self around autonomy and independence and I consequently value those characteristics in others, the likelihood is that I will have tension if not outright difficulty collaborating with someone who does not exhibit behaviors I associate with those qualities or who does not place the same value on them in my opinion. I may judge them to be incompetent or unmotivated and lazy; I may try to get them to buy into my belief of the importance of autonomy, or I may simply not trust that they will get things done and just do things myself. Whatever my response, I will only minimally, if at all, recognize and value any contribution they might be able to make to a joint effort.

Or perhaps I've built my identity on timeliness and order. I will then have trouble working with someone who is more lax about time and pays less attention to orderliness. Similarly, I may believe I'm competent and powerful, or relatively incapable and powerless and feel challenged by someone I perceive to believe differently about themselves. Whatever the core aspects around which I've formed my sense of self, the potential for miscommunication and failed collaboration will increase when I need to work with someone who has adopted different core aspects. As with differences in more general funds of knowledge, not recognizing or addressing these differences easily sabotages communication and collaboration.

Perceptions of and understanding of power. In some ways the most complex source of differences that challenge communication and collaboration is perceptions of and understanding of power (i.e., how I define power, how I believe power is gained or lost, who I believe has power). This area is often the least explicitly addressed in communication and collaboration. Yet, how we perceive and understand power has substantial influence on the success or lack of success of communication and collaboration.

It is common, at least in the U.S., to assume a universal definition of power as power *over*, be this over our selves, others or our social, work-related or natural environments. We often also tend to blur distinctions between having power and being competent. Consequently, we exert a great deal of time and energy in learning about and acquiring mastery in areas important to us; i.e., becoming competent, acquiring power in that area. We structure our communication and collaboration efforts in service of such mastery and tend to disrespect those we believe do not exhibit similar mastery.

There is, however, another less-well recognized definition of power: power as power *for*. This is definition is much less common in the U.S., but is one clearly captured in the Spanish translation for power: *poder*. *Poder* refers not just to power over as understood in English but also to power *for*, or capacity, as in "Yo puedo" ("I can"). Jaworski (2011) makes an interesting point that implies this definition of power: "The facilitator who has done the interior work will 'set the field' for the participants and help them learn the way into that deeper territory through disciplined personal practice" (p. 85).

An important aspect of how individuals perceive and define power is the "model of agency" they hold (Markus and Kitayama, 2003). Models of agency can be put into one of three groups: independent, relational-interpersonal, and contractual-structural (Barrera & Kramer, 2009). These models define four aspects of our actions: their "goodness," consequences, style and sources. It is the latter aspect—the sources of our actions—that is most relevant to the definition of power as discussed here.[3]

From the perspective of someone who holds an <u>independent model of agency</u>, actions are perceived as contingent only on the preferences and motives of the doer of those actions. Power, thus, lies in the doer's ability to select and control his or her actions. In contrast, someone holding a <u>relational-interactional model of agency</u> believes that actions are, or should be, jointly determined and controlled according to the nature of their relationship with those with whom they are interacting (e.g., my actions toward someone would depend on whether or not they are family, for instance). In this case, power is jointly held and is not individually controllable. Finally, a <u>contractual-structural model of agency</u> holds that actions are, or should be, responsive to social roles and obligations independent of either individual mastery or given relationships. It is the group or groups within which a person operates that hold the power to determine actions in any given instance (e.g., a city government).

Many of us operate from more than one model depending on the context of a given interaction. We recognize, for example, that it is a court that holds the power in certain interactions (<u>contractual-structural model of agency</u>). In other collaborative situations, on the other hand, we recognize that power is not solely in the hands of one person (<u>relational-interactional model of agency</u>). Nevertheless, in most cases one model will tend to be our "go to" model when possible.

<u>Activity</u>: Given these models of agency, the following questions can provide insight into our understanding of power. Reflect on each one and discuss with at least one other person.

1. Do I see those with whom I seek to communicate or collaborate as holding the same, more, or less power? Why or why not?
2. In what situations do I believe I am competent? Powerful? Skilled? Unskilled? Incompetent? Why or why not?
3. How do I express and maintain power? Which model of agency do I tend to favor?
4. To what degree am I conscious of power in my communication and collaboration with others?
5. What have been my experiences with power *over* in communication and collaboration? With power *for*? What are the differences? How did I feel?

Given the scope of this text, differences in perceptions and understandings of power, as well as differences in funds of knowledge and sense of self vis-à-vis our understanding of diversity can be only be briefly addressed in this chapter. They will be further addressed, albeit more indirectly, in Part II, as well as in Part III. Readers are also referred to Barrera, I., Corso, R., & Macpherson, D., 2003 and Barrera & Kramer, 2009, which address differences in funds of knowledge, sense of self and perceptions of power in more detail.

Responses to diversity

It is not enough to recognize the source of the diversity between individuals. It is possible to realize that someone has very different funds of knowledge from our own or operates with a different model of agency yet respond to that realization in ways that do not foster optimum communication or collaboration. One person might, for example, acknowledge differences in funds of knowledge yet not be able to connect them with their own funds of knowledge in any meaningful way. This person would simply each leave them side-by-side. For purposes of this discussion, we'll call this type of response an

A and B response. Unfortunately, an A and B response can all too easily deteriorate into A vs. B response where the differences are not only responded to as separate but also as contradictory or antagonistic.

A second type of response is one where someone both acknowledges and joins the differences in some meaningful way (A joined with B). This latter response goes beyond simply placing differences side by side, whether with or against each other. It perceives differences as complementary and connects them in ways that bring out what they hold in common as well as what is unique about each.

The first response, A and B can reflect the belief that differences do not affect available resources or options. It can also, if the differences are perceived as contradictory, reflect the belief that they subtract from available resources and options. Such a response can easily lead to miscommunications and ineffective or unrealized collaboration efforts for the simple reason that it implicitly or explicitly places differences on an either-or continuum (e.g., I can value or choose either A or B). This type of response makes engagement in authentic collaboration very difficult.

In contrast, an A joined with B response reflects the belief that differences can not only co-exist, they can also enrich and add to each other while retaining their uniqueness. An A joined with B response goes beyond placing differences side-by-side or making them contradictory. A joined with B responses seek to integrate differences in ways that leverage their unique strengths while simultaneously honoring what they hold in common.

In our own work on Skilled Dialogue we have distilled four underlying beliefs associated with people who regularly responded to differences from an A joined with B perspective. These were people who communicated effectively and regularly achieved authentic collaboration with others who held views and beliefs different from their own.[4]

Differences simply make people different. The first belief was the belief that differences do not make people right or wrong; they simply make people different. Effective communicators and collaborators recognized that the "rightness" or "wrongness" of these differences, like all differences, is dependent on the context in which they are found. It is that context that dictates the effectiveness (i.e., "rightness") of a particular view or belief as well as its morality (i.e., social or religious value).

Individuals' views and beliefs are evidence-based. Effective communicators and collaborators believed that a person holding a particular view or belief and behaving in a way commensurate with that value or belief did so based on experience and other data that validated that view or belief. Perceiving differences in this way allowed them to affirm the person(s) with whom they wished to communicate and collaborate as capable and, consequently, led to treating them as such.[5] This belief does not negate the judgment that particular behavior(s) or beliefs were dysfunctional or life threatening nor does it negate the need for legal procedures when necessary. It does allow for respectful interaction with a person exhibiting those behaviors or beliefs (i.e., as a person whose behaviors and beliefs are the results of an intact learning capability rather than as a person who was ignorant, incapable, or willfully deviated from particular norms and thus establish respect while simultaneously).[6]

Diversity of views and beliefs adds to existing options and resources. Effective communicators and collaborators echoed the understanding that "Life relies on diversity to give it the possibility of adapting to changing conditions. …Where there is diversity …innovative solutions are created all the time, just because different people do things differently" (Wheatley, 2005, p. 78). They tended to believe strongly that they could learn from those different from themselves; i.e., that diversity added to rather than diminished options and resources. They understood that the exploration of views that were novel to them could generate previously unimagined resources and options.

Differences are complementary. For effective communicators and collaborators the belief that differences can be complementary rather than contradictory flowed naturally from the previous one. Individuals who tended to use A joined with B responses to diversity believed that differences, when joined, could reveal a whole (C) larger than the sum of its parts (A and B). Nothing was lost and much could be gained from integrating differences. This fourth belief is the essence of paradox, which is the focus of Chapter 2.

Discussion Questions/Activities

1. Make a list of words you associate with differences (e.g., exciting, troublesome). What can you conclude about your perception of differences based on this list?
2. What types of differences do you find positive (e.g., being talented)? What types of differences do you find negative (e.g., lack of punctuality)? Can you find a common theme to each group?
3. What are some important aspects of your sense of self? Find at least one other person to discuss the similarities and differences between their sense of self and yours.
4. List at least three things that you assume everyone knows are necessary to successful communicating and collaborating. Reality check this list with at least three other people with whom you have collaborated: ask them if they agree or disagree.

Chapter 2

Paradox

"In human life…, there can be no real unity except through the awareness of real divisions. (Needleman. 2003)

Differences can be perceived as contradictory (i.e., divisive) and as complementary (i.e., in unity, adding to and augmenting). Both perceptions can be useful depending on the context in which they are chosen. Which perception we choose in any given interaction will have a significant impact on communication and collaboration with people who hold views and beliefs different from our own. Our choice will determine whether we can achieve "collaborative intelligence," a term used by two authors to emphasize the need to focus on how differences can work for rather than against us.[7] The concept of paradox is key to this focus. When understood through the lens of paradox, the distinctions between realities need neither be erased nor polarized into contradictions. They can, rather, be integrated and placed within a relationship where they can complement each other while retaining their distinctions.

Science is indicating that we are all genetically wired to perceive reality in binary pairs. Polarizing these pairs into exclusive opposites, however, appears to be more of a culturally rooted tendency (Newberg, D'Aquili, & Rause, 2001), especially in the West. As a result, we tend to find it difficult to think or even imagine differences as components of a single reality. When held together in this fashion, differences generate complementary energy like the poles of a battery. It is this sense of diversity held in paradox that allows for dialogue in which differences work for us and we need neither abandon nor compromise one set of beliefs or views for the sake of another.

A paradoxical understanding of differences is grounded in the integration of diverse realities (i.e., beliefs, perspectives, behaviors) into an inclusive whole where each plays a necessary role. It allows for the creation of a joint space that integrates contrasting perspectives. Graphically, this space can be thought of as the circle that joins the black and white spaces depicted by a yin/yang symbol (see Part III for illustration). Within this joint space the riches of contrasting views (e.g., black and white) can be simultaneously accessed.

The joint space created by paradox is called 3rd Space within Skilled Dialogue. It is specifically defined as a conceptual, relational, and emotional space within which differences are integrated to generate a *sum* that is more than each individual component without compromising their distinctive features.[8] An imperfect analogy can be made in relation to colors. Green, for example, is the *sum*, or 3rd Space, of blue and yellow. It requires that blue remain blue and yellow remain yellow unlike gray, which compromises black and white, requiring either the darkening of white or the lightening of black.

3rd Space is inclusive of differences. If, for example, we think about one person's views and beliefs (A) being in one space and another's different views and beliefs (B) in a second space, then 3rd Space would be the common space created *by the removal of the wall (but not the boundaries) between the two original spaces.* That is, the distinctions between the A and B remain but are not perceived as contradictory. Nothing is removed from either. Neither A nor B need to move; neither, however, is the newly created joint space merely the two original spaces side by side. In the removing the wall between them, each becomes larger, able to encompass and tap into what had previously been unavailable (i.e., on the other side of the wall).

3rd Space, this common space that bridges differences, is often the most challenging aspect of Skilled Dialogue for its users to understand. It is, however, merely the reality of the old adage: the whole is greater than the sum of its parts. A body, for example, is more than just the aggregate of limbs and organs "side by side." An arm becomes more when attached to a body yet still remains distinct as an arm. Using a different metaphor, a choir is more than the simple aggregate of individual voices side by side yet, everyone retains their individual voice. Both aspects—the "more" and the unchanged uniqueness—are key to collaboration as conceptualized by Skilled Dialogue. It is collaboration that is more than just working together in parallel, each person working on their own project or one person assisting another without adding his or her own contributions.

This integrative perspective of differences distinguishes 3rd Space from other more common either-or perspectives. It also differentiates it from both-and perspectives with which it is sometimes confused. The former places differences into contradictory frames; the latter places differences side-by-side but does not integrate them to create a more inclusive reality. The historical reality of separate but equal schools is an example of a both-and perspective. The intent, however imperfectly achieved, was to give those schools equal value yet stop short of actual integration.

Holding differences in paradox (i.e., creating 3rd Space) is, for most of us, a skill that takes time to learn. Further explanations and examples are provided in Parts II and III of this text. The purpose of this chapter is only to introduce paradox and 3rd Space as core concepts of Skilled Dialogue. Toward this end, two additional points are addressed below: the contrast between diversity understood with and without the lens of paradox and the role of paradox in *setting the stage for miracles.*

Understanding diversity with and without the lens of paradox. Without the lens of paradox, our understanding of differences tends to be subtractive: bringing in something different means losing or diminishing what already exists. And, often, we do not wish or are not ready to have what we are familiar with lost or diminished, especially when we cannot identify a perceptible advantage. It's OK to lose crawling, for example, as walking offers greater mobility. But what if what we believe must be diminished or replaced is a familiar belief or way of behaving that has served us for years? How fully are we willing to collaborate if we believe that collaboration involves the loss of what we believe is important or true or best?

Without the lens of paradox, diversity offers at best only differences that, even when acknowledged as equally valid, must always remain separate. At worst, it necessitates the sacrifice of one perspective in favor of another—and the consequent lose of any benefits that perspective might offer. Without the lens of paradox there can be no creation of a larger whole within which diverse perspectives can be maintained and mined for their individual strengths. Without the lens of paradox, communication and collaboration across differences offers only two choices: compromising the views or perspectives of one person to accommodate the other or selecting one view or perspective at the expense of the contrasting view or perspective.

With the lens of paradox, however, a third choice becomes possible: the integration of differences into a whole greater than their sum without losing their individual uniqueness. Each difference can be acknowledged as valid, yielding both the benefits of each and the benefits of their integration.

Parallel play and cooperative play, two descriptions of play in early childhood education, may perhaps clarify these statements further. Parallel play is when two children sit side-by-side playing with the same materials yet sharing their play minimally if at all. Neither child takes the other's actions into account unless they actively interfere with their own. Little if any communication is required except in instances where actions need to be defended or toys need to be acquired. So too, when differences are understood outside the lens of paradox, communication is primarily used in self-interest to emphasize or defend. At best compromise, which withholds acceptance from the whole of either view, may be sought. In contrast, cooperative play involves two children cplaying with a single set of toys. Each takes the other's actions into account and adds to or otherwise responds to those actions, ending up with a creation that no single child would have developed in isolation.

Another example is that of a musical chord. A chord is composed of multiple notes played simultaneously without changing their individual tones. It includes multiple notes yet also creates a sound distinct from any of the notes played individually. Similarly, the lens of paradox allows differences to be leveraged in service of a larger whole rather than minimized or eliminated altogether. It makes it possible to go beyond merely co-existing to actually uniting diverse strengths toward a common end just as individual notes can be integrated into a chord. It is in so doing that paradox sets the stage for miracles.

How paradox sets the stage for "miracles. As put by Jaworski (1996), "What is 'miraculous' might be just what is beyond our current understanding" (p. 14). Skilled Dialogue uses the word "miracles" in this sense, referring to outcomes other than those predicted by a person's current understanding of a particular situation or interaction. In entertaining the possibility of a sum larger than the individual differences (i.e., parts) while retaining the uniqueness of those differences, paradox sets the stage for miracles by stimulating understandings of relationships between differences in ways beyond someone's original understanding of those differences.

The use of paradox in this sense is extensively addressed in *Paradoxical Thinking: How to Profit from Your Contradictions*. In this book Fletcher and Olwyler (1997) affirm the need for a key aspect of paradox: *perception shifting*. "Perception shifting calls for "breaking open …narrow judgments about the positive or negative value of… contradictory qualities" (p. 3). When our perception of certain qualities (e.g., procrastination) remains negative, we are likely to perceive them only in contradiction to qualities we perceive as positive. We are unlikely to call upon those qualities in any constructive way. When on the other hand, our perception shifts and our judgment of a quality as negative breaks open, we can call on that quality to achieve something positive (e.g., mindfulness).

Perception shifting is a first step in setting the stage for miracles (i.e., moving beyond our current understanding) within Skilled Dialogue. When, for example, I am no longer judging others' diverse perspectives or beliefs as negative in comparison to mine, I become open to perceiving the strengths of those perspectives and beliefs and, consequently, to integrating their strengths with my own to generate creative and unanticipated collaborative outcomes. Further discussion and concrete examples of perception shifting and paradox in relation to interpersonal differences are given in Part III.

Discussion Questions/Activities

1. What is your understanding of "paradox"? Discuss the concept with others; identify at least three examples of paradox.

2. Read and discuss the following quote: "We split paradoxes so reflexively that we do not understand the price we pay for our habit. The poles of a paradox are like the poles of a battery: hold them together, and they generate the energy of life; pull them apart, and the current stops flowing. When we separate any of the profound paired truths of our lives, both poles become lifeless as well. Dissecting a living paradox has the same impact on our intellection, emotional, and spiritual well-being as the decision to breathe in without ever breathing in would have on our physical health" (Palmer, 1997, p. 64)

3. Think of a recent interaction with someone whose views were different from your own. Discuss how your diverse views could both be true and even complement each other.

4. Has your perception of any behavior or belief ever shifted changed? Describe what occurred.

Chapter 3

Dialogue and Skilled Dialogue

"I therefore recommend that you and the other side establish a 'brave space,' a learning environment that emboldens you to embrace [differences], take personal risks, and reconsider perspectives." (Shapiro, 2017)

Skilled Dialogue is a dialogic approach to communication and collaboration that leverages diversity's positive contributions to communication and collaboration. As such it has many elements in common with dialogue in general.

Dialogue

There are many ways to describe dialogue. One writer describes it as "a *conversation with a center, not sides* …a way of taking the energy of our differences and channeling it toward something that has never been created before" (Isaacs, 1999, p. 19). This statement captures two critical aspects of dialogue: a focus on a common center rather than sides, and the channeling of energy toward what has never been created before.

Dialogue honors differences deeply. By focusing on the flow of energy between people rather than on static positions (e.g., your view, my view), it seeks to reconcile diverse and even seemingly contradictory viewpoints in order to tap their strengths and achieve inclusive resolutions. This focus contrasts dialogue with other forms of interaction such as discussion, which aims to simply express diverse viewpoints; conflict resolution, which seeks to reach non-inclusive resolution of differences; or debate, which focuses on listening for flaws or weaknesses in one perspective as compared to another. An in-depth description of dialogue can be found in the ten Dialogue Principles, or Dialogue Decalogue, formulated by L. Swidler (www.dialogueinstitute.org).

Skilled Dialogue

Three elements distilled from these principles are relevant to Skilled Dialogue:

1. Dialogue is a process that can only take place between equals seeking to learn with and from each other rather than to teach or persuade.
2. Dialogue requires a basis of trust to be successful.
3. Dialogue entails experiencing others' perspectives subjectively, as if they reflected our own, rather than objectively as if they were entirely detached from our own.

These elements underscore the three qualities associated with Skilled Dialogue (see Table 3.1). The following brief discussion introduces these qualities. Each is more specifically addressed in Part II.

Respect. Respect may be described as the explicit verbal and nonverbal acknowledgment that another's identity is evidence-based and deserves to be honored as such. Sarah Lawrence-Lightfoot's words, cited in our earlier Skilled Dialogue book, are still relevant to our definition of respect: "Making oneself vulnerable is an act of trust and respect, as is receiving and honoring the vulnerability of another. Such an offering of oneself aligns with Martin Buber's idea that a person who says 'You' does not 'have' something, but [rather] 'stands in relation' " (p. 93, 1999).

At its core, respect is about just that: "standing in relation" to those with whom we interact. So often in interactions, especially those with others who hold perspectives and beliefs different from our own, we lose this relational focus and instead pay attention only to the ideas and positions involved. When this is the case, we stand in relation not to the person with whom we are interacting but only to "objective" ideas and positions.

Reciprocity. Reciprocity is a corollary quality to respect. It involves the recognition that another's identity is of equal importance to our own and, consequently, merits equal expression. More succinctly, reciprocity is about creating interactional symmetry so that one person's voice (i.e., power) does not ignore or overshadow another's. At the core of reciprocity is the recognition that each person in an interaction is equally capable and equally powerful. To understand reciprocity in this sense is to distinguish between power *over* and power *for*. The former assumes an understanding of power as greater force or authority; the latter assumes an understanding of power as capacity or capability. This distinction is perhaps clearer in Spanish. The word for power, *poder*, can be used not only as in English to mean "power;" it can also be used as a verb to mean "I am able" as in "*yo puedo*" (i.e., I can). It is in this latter sense that dialogue in general and Skilled Dialogue in particular understand reciprocity.

Reciprocity does not require denying that one person may have more expertise, knowledge or authority than another in particular areas. It does require (a) recognizing that everyone's experience and perceptions are of equal value, though they may well have resulted in perspectives and beliefs contrary to our own, and (b) acknowledging that every person brings an equal capacity to learn and to act. These two requirements establish a base for the crafting of interactions within which all participants can contribute meaningfully and make willing choices rather than forced either-or choices. In reciprocal interactions one point of view neither dominates nor excludes diverse points of view.

Responsiveness. Responsiveness is a quality that becomes possible only when both respect and reciprocity are present. Respect is about honoring boundaries. Reciprocity is about honoring the expression of those boundaries. Responsiveness is about responding to that expression in ways that communicate our understanding and affirmation of it. Responding and being responsive are not the same, however. Responsiveness refers to more than merely giving a response. It refers to the tenor of that response. Is it a response that only acknowledges that we spoke or is it a response that communicates understanding and valuing of the perspective expressed, no matter how diverse? We give a response, but we *become* responsive.

Remem (2000) describes her shift from simply responding to becoming responsive: "So I no longer have theories about people. I don't diagnose them or decide what their problem is. I simply meet with them and listen. As we sit together, I don't even have an agenda, but I know that something will emerge from our conversation over time that is a part of a larger coherent pattern that neither of us can fully see at the moment." (p.90, 2000).

A relatively superficial example may serve to further clarify the role and impact of respect, reciprocity and responsiveness on interactions. As a young professional not yet having developed Skilled Dialogue, I (Barrera) was involved in putting on an institute in central Texas under the guidance of an out-of-state team. During the process I mentioned to the team leader that I'd be so glad to see it rain so our humidity would finally clear out. The team leader immediately invalidated my statement—and myself as well—by laughing and saying that rain didn't lower humidity; it elevated it. Though he responded to my comment, he was not at all responsive. His reply invalidated both whom I was and what I knew as a long time Texas resident.

Unfortunately his is not an atypical reaction to diverse perspectives. It was neither responsive nor respectful or reciprocal. First, there was no acknowledgement that my identity (i.e., who I was as I spoke those words) was evidence-based or that it deserved to be honored, two essential aspects of respect. This would not necessarily have meant that he needed to acknowledge I was right and he was wrong—only to acknowledge that we had two very different perspectives based on our very different geographical contexts and experiences.[9] Even a "Why do you think that?" would have been more respectful in that it would have implied that I was not just ignorant of reality.

Second, the lack of acknowledgement of my identity prevented any reciprocity. My voice was, quite literally, dismissed. Not only did he accord greater power to his knowledge than to mine, he also took for granted that he didn't need to understand my view or ask if there was any validity to it. Third, while the leader did respond to my statement, he was not responsive to my perspective. He took only his perspective into account and showed neither curiosity nor any interest in the fact that I held a different perspective. His reply did not take my words or me into account in any way other than to invalidate both.

Looking back I realize that this interaction repeated a pattern that occurred throughout the institute. We did continue to communicate and collaborate—it was my job to do so after all. My participation and learning, however, were not quite what they might have been, and, I wonder if perhaps the participation and learning of the institute participants were also less than they might have been had a respectful, reciprocal and responsive pattern of communication and collaboration been in place.

The fact that I still remember that interaction and how I felt after over 30 years speaks to the power of communication and collaboration without respect, reciprocity or responsiveness. It was as I sought to explore that power across a wide range of professional contexts that I began to develop the Skilled Dialogue approach and then to work with Dr. Kramer in refining and field-testing it.

Skilled Dialogue Elements

Skilled Dialogue is a field-tested interactional approach that seeks to craft respectful, reciprocal and responsive interactions across diverse perspectives. Its ultimate goal is to transform and integrate apparent contradictions between perspectives so that differences can unite and inspire rather than separate and invalidate. It is composed of two dispositions and six strategies. These elements give concrete form to the qualities of respect, responsiveness and reciprocity just discussed (see Table 3.2).

Through these dispositions and qualities, Skilled Dialogue structures interactions in ways that tap into diversity's potential to enrich available options and opportunities without either sacrificing or compromising the differences involved (Barrera, I., Corso, R., & Macpherson, D., 2003; Barrera, I., Kramer, L., & Macpherson, D., 2012; Barrera, I. & Kramer, L., 2009). It is important to note, however, that Skilled Dialogue is not designed for interactions involving threats of any sort, interactions with people with serious mental or cognitive impairments that inhibit their ability to assess reality,[10] or interactions where minimal interaction is required. Individuals are encouraged to choose it only in situations where both time and commitment are important or necessary.

The following examples from the authors and other individuals to whom they have taught Skilled Dialogue are illustrative of situations in which Skilled Dialogue has been used successfully to transform contradictions and unite both diverse perspectives and the people who held them:

(1) When a supervisor asked me to do something that I believed compromised my sense of who I was and how I wanted to work,

(2) When I didn't feel that the other person understood my point of view or took it into account,

(3) When I wanted to collaborate with someone and they didn't seem to carry their weight,

(4) When I needed to talk with someone I was supervising about a troublesome behavior,

(5) When I felt I had to give up "me" in order to succeed at work.

Skilled Dialogue Dispositions. Skilled Dialogue is grounded in two dispositions: Choosing Relationship over Control and Setting the Stage for Miracles. Choosing Relationship over Control taps the power of the other. It is a disposition toward joining (i.e., relating) differences rather than polarizing (i.e., dividing) them into either-or dichotomies.

Skilled Dialogue's second disposition, Setting the Stage for Miracles, leverages this interconnectivity through tapping into the power of paradox. It is through this power that we integrate differences so as to unite the power of the other with our own to generate outcomes not predictable from existing data (i.e., miracles).

Skilled Dialogue Strategies. Skilled Dialogue's six strategies emerge from the intersection between its qualities and its dispositions. Read from the top down Table 3.2 identifies the strategies associated with each disposition. The strategies of *Welcoming*, *Sense-Making*, and *Joining* express the disposition of Choosing Relationship over Control. They are designed to tap into the power of the other vis-à-vis our own. The strategies of

Allowing, Appreciating, and *Harmonizing* express the disposition of Setting the Stage for Miracles and tap into the power of paradox.

Read from left to right, Table 3.2 shows the relationship between the strategies and the qualities of respect, reciprocity and responsiveness. *Welcoming* and *Allowing* are designed to express respect thru honoring identity. *Sense-Making* and *Appreciating* seek to establish reciprocity by honoring voice. And, finally, *Joining* and *Harmonizing* culminate the Skilled Dialogue process by establishing responsiveness through honoring connection.

Chapters 5-7 examine each of the Skilled Dialogue elements in detail. Additionally, Chapter 9 provides examples and non-examples of each strategy. Chapter 10 then returns to a global picture of Skilled Dialogue by providing examples of various scenarios to illustrate all of its elements in practice.

Discussion Questions/Activities

1. How would you distinguish between Skilled Dialogue's 3 R's: respect, reciprocity, and responsiveness? Provide an example and non-example of each quality?

2. Have you ever felt that, though someone responded to you they were not responsive? Discuss your experience.

3. How do you understand dialogue in your personal communication? Provide and discuss an example of dialogue you might have that is "a *conversation with a center, not sides* …a way of taking the energy of our differences and channeling it toward something that has never been created before" (Isaacs, p. 19).

4. Describe a <u>dialogue</u> and a <u>discussion</u>. What is the difference?

5. Think about the three interactive qualities essential for Skilled Dialogue to realize its full potential across differences. Discuss why each quality is critical for optimal interactions.

6. How would you explain the two dispositions underlying of Skilled Dialogue? Discuss how each is critical to successful Skilled Dialogue.

7. Discuss Skilled Dialogue's six strategies. Explain how each strategy "simultaneously deepens and extends the other strategies."

Table 3.1. Skilled Dialogue's Qualities

RESPECT *Honors identity* *(Welcoming + Allowing)* **(ABOUT RECOGNIZING BOUNDARIES)**	<u>Key Questions:</u> *Do my interactions acknowledge the diverse ways in which others perceive & structure their world/experiences?* *Am I avoiding polarization of perspectives and staying with the tension of contradictory beliefs, values, and behaviors "(i.e., culture bumps")?*
RECIPROCITY *Honors voice* *(Sense-Making + Appreciating)* **(ABOUT VALUING OTHER'S VOICE AND CONTRIBUTIONS)**	<u>Key Questions:</u> *Am I inviting other to "tell their story" (i.e., describe their perspective(s) and truly listening?* *Am I attending to others' stories with wonder and curiosity enough to recognize "rightness" or "gift" of their perspective ("story") in relation to my own?*
RESPONSIVENESS *Honors connection* *(Joining + Harmonizing)* **(ABOUT BEING OPEN TO "NOT KNOWING")**	<u>Key Questions:</u> *How aware am I of what limits or obstructs my ability/willingness to respond in meaningful ways to other?* *Am I exploring how diverse perspectives are complementary with the intent to better perceive the greater more inclusive "frame" that unites them?*

Table 3.2. Skilled Dialogue Elements

	Dispositions	
	Tapping the Power of the Other: Choosing Relationship over Control	Tapping the Power of Paradox: Setting the Stage for Miracles
Qualities	**Strategies**	
RESPECT *Honoring Identity THRU Explicit Acknowledgment of Boundaries*	*Welcoming* Hallmark: Positive regard of other Critical Question: Am I looking forward to this interaction confident that I'll learn something new?	*Allowing:* Hallmark: Expression of other's perspective w/o contradictory remarks or defense of mine Critical Question: Am I willing to listen to other without needing to defend my views?
RECIPROCITY *Honoring Voice THRU Affirmation of IAll Person's Equal "Power for"*	*Sense-Making:* Hallmark: Understanding positive role of other's perspective in their lives Critical Question: Can I find how the other's perspective makes sense?	*Appreciating:* Hallmark: Expressed awareness of what I can learn from other Critical Question: Am I willing to appreciate the value of the other's perspective?

	Joining:	Harmonizing:
RESPONSIVENESS *Honoring Connection* *THRU* *Linking & Integrating* *Differences*	<u>Hallmark</u>: Representation of other's perspective such that the other can say "That's it; you've got it" <u>Critical Question</u>: Can I credibly restate the other's perspective as if it were mine?	<u>Hallmark</u>: Integration of other's perspective with my own to generate inclusive response options <u>Critical Question</u>: Can I find a "3rd choice" inclusive of both my and other's perspectives?

PART II:
SKILLED DIALOGUE ELEMENTS

Chapter 4

Skilled Dialogue Dispositions: Leveraging the Power of the Other and the Power of Paradox

Human dispositions are unique and personal qualities. They are internal tendencies, beliefs and meanings that provide the source of an individual's thoughts, feelings and actions. (Usher, Usher, & Usher, 2003)

The importance of dispositions to the quality and outcome of communication and collaboration cannot be overstated. Dispositions determine *how* we do what we do. They are about the inner state or intent that underlies our actions and words and significantly affects what those actions and words communicate. The same actions or words can communicate two quite different things depending on the disposition underlying them. "I am so proud of you" can, for example, communicate sarcasm or a compliment, influencing our response to those words as well as to the person saying them.

Research into perception and interactions seems to indicate that an individual can perceive, albeit unconsciously, what another is disposed to do before any action is taken (Iacoboni, 2009). Rizzolatti, Fogassi, and Gallese (2006), for example, discovered that an observer's brain could mirror the intent of another's actions even before that action was completed. When, for example, a researcher reached for a glass to pick it up rather than to throw it away, a monkey's brain accurately mirrored that specific intent. This mirroring is also reflected anecdotally in an interesting phenomenon experienced by drivers. Have you ever "known" that the driver ahead of you was going to turn before they actually turned or gave any signal of turning? Though the formal evidence for this phenomenon is not yet substantial, it nevertheless seems likely that the dispositions with which we undertake an action, whether spoken or not, will be clear to those with whom we interact before we actually perform that action.

Skilled Dialogue's unique identity and power is shaped by two particular dispositions. We (the authors) have named these descriptively: Choosing Relationship Over Control and Setting the Stage for Miracles. The first of these is designed to leverage the power of the relational field that exists between individuals, what Cloud (2016) terms "the power of the other." The second leverages this interconnectivity through tapping into the power of paradox.

Our research and practice have shown that the strengths of diverse perspectives and beliefs are most easily accessed and integrated when these dispositions underlie the Skilled Dialogue strategies. The discussion of each disposition that follows provides a meaningful context for the discussion of these strategies in Chapters 5-7.

Choosing Relationship over Control

Skilled Dialogue's disposition of Choosing Relationship over Control sets a platform for leveraging the relationship between diverse perspectives in communicative and collaborative interactions. More specifically, Choosing Relationship over Control explicitly affirms this relationship by affirming the "power of the other," a term used by Cloud (2016) to refer to how relationships shape and influence our own beliefs and actions.

Choosing Relationship over Control should not, however, be interpreted to mean that relationship and control are oppositional or contradictory choices. Neither can replace the other. Both are, like a hammer and an ax, useful at different times and for different purposes. For purposes of mutual communication and collaboration that is respectful, reciprocal and responsive, we believe that choosing relationship is the most appropriate and efficacious choice.

Control, as used in the title of this disposition, refers not just to controlling other's actions or choices. It also refers to control of other aspects of communicative interactions such as control of knowledge (e.g., this knowledge should prevail over that knowledge because it's truer or better), control of situations (e.g., things must happen or be done this way and only this way in order to meet X goal), and control of time (e.g., appointment times that are non-negotiable, unilaterally set agendas). While these aspects of control are often subtle and unconscious, their power to disrupt relationship (i.e., sabotage the power of the other) is as strong if not stronger than that of more explicit forms of control.

Choosing control as meant within Skilled Dialogue means entering into an interaction with a singular vision focused on and invested in only one view or perspective and one predefined outcome (i.e., entering into an interaction certain we know best with no allowance for how or what another might contribute.

In contrast, choosing relationship, as understood in Skilled Dialogue, involves entering into an interaction knowing we don't always know best and making allowance for "the power of the other," (i.e., how the other person might add to or enrich our own perspectives). It means entering into an interaction with binocular vision, invested in both how our perspective *and* the perspective of the person with whom we are interacting might be meaningfully related and, indeed, mutually beneficial.

<u>Choosing interpersonal relationship</u>. Choosing Relationship over Control vis-à-vis relationship with others is about shifting the focus of interpersonal interactions from I-It interactions to I-Thou interactions. Making this shift moves interactions into a context within which diverse identities, voices and connections can be honored. "A defining quality of I-Thou engagement is 'feeling felt' … At such moments we sense that the other person knows how we feel, and so we feel known [i.e., respected and responded to]." I-It, on the other hand, involves "thinking *about* the other person rather than attuning to her" (Goleman, 2006, pp. 107, 109).

Remen's (2000) comments are relevant to this distinction "… knowing where we are going encourages us to stop seeing and hearing and allows us to fall asleep...[such knowing allows] a part of [us] to rush ahead to [our destination] the moment [we] see it" (p. 289). She illustrates these words further through a cautionary tale about an encounter with a young physician. This physician had learned after the death of one of his long-time patients that she (the patient) had been a great Navajo medicine woman. He tells Remen that he learned this from a researcher writing a book about American Indian medicine traditions. This researcher had been led to the physician as he sought out the woman because he believed that she "would have the answers he needed" (p. 69). Remen then recounts the physician sadly telling her that, though he had treated this woman for many years, he had been so preoccupied with numbers and tests that he had remained unaware of her skill as a renowned medicine woman. The physician ends his conversation by saying "What I would give for even one hour with her now, to ask her any of my unanswered questions...Or simply to ask for her blessing' " (p. 69). From a Skilled Dialogue perspective, that last poignant statement might be translated as "What I would give to have chosen to enter into relationship with this woman rather than to only seek to control her illnesses."

Choosing Relationship over Control predisposes us to accommodate, and at times even bypass, generic information and interactions to relate with an individual's unique identity, strengths and needs rather than to merely design interactions according to generic or preset agendas. Yet, it in no way excludes objective knowledge such as the physician's in Remen's story. Rather, Choosing Relationship over Control seeks relational subjective knowledge as a context for interpreting that objective knowledge. The reality is that each type of knowledge, relational and objective, has both advantages and limitations. Learning about hearts in general, for example, has greatly enhanced medical practice and saved many lives. Learning about my own particular heart, though, can save my life.

Unfortunately, being disposed to choose relationship over control is often not our first impulse, especially when interacting with individuals whose perspectives and beliefs differ significantly from our own. Our typical patterns of interacting with these individuals tend to be more tactical (i.e., focused on how) than relational (i.e., focused on who).

"We sift through others' views for what we can make use to make our own points [or to reach our preset goals]. We measure success by how effective we have been in gaining advantage for our favored positions" (Senge, as quoted in Kahane, 2004, p. x). In other words, we choose control over relationship.

In contrast, the goal of Choosing Relationship over Control is on *who*, not how. It focuses on understanding the meaning of *this* perspective or behavior exhibited by *this* person in *this* situation. Consequently, in many instances Choosing Relationship over Control provides what might be considered less stable, "softer" data than objective "scientific" knowledge. While the latter may be more truthful in relation to the "average" or generic individual, the former is always more truthful in relation to a particular individual.

Choosing Relationship over Control creates a personal and personalized context within which knowledge becomes about someone whom we actually know and are in relationship with. It becomes about *Jack*, for example, not just about an impersonal other in front of me. As one writer put it more than two decades ago, relational knowledge "...arises not from standing back in order to look at [and control], but by active and intentional engagement" (Groome, 1980, p. 141).

<u>Choosing relationship between dispositions and views</u>. Beyond disposing us to relationships with another, Choosing Relationship over Control is also grounded in a more general understanding of the universe itself as relational. When we neglect this second aspect, we miss seeing how diverse perspectives and beliefs are related and instead see them only as separate and even as oppositional, entirely overlooking what those diverse perspective and beliefs might enrich our interaction.

Part of the difficulty in shifting from control to relationship is that a disposition toward choosing control emphasizes certainty and predictability, characteristics with which we are, typically, more comfortable. We act, explicitly or implicitly, to maintain that certainty and predictability by establishing this-is-better-than-that hierarchies. On the other hand, because of its acceptance of unique rather than generic realities, a disposition toward choosing relationship over control favors uncertainty and unpredictability. It not only fosters a plurality of possibilities, it also and perhaps more significantly, fosters possibilities we might not ever have imagined. With this disposition our understanding of reality, like our understanding of a single person, softens and becomes open and flexible rather than rigid and fixed.

Choosing Relationship over Control brings knowledge of diverse perspectives and beliefs from the outside in (i.e., from looking at or reading about them to engaging with them in some way). In contemporary society, this distinction is not always as clear as it might seem. It is somewhat similar to going from 2-D movies to 3-D movies. More currently, it might be more like going from either of those to virtual reality. A recent news report illustrates the impact of this latter transition well. Gabo Arora, a UN senior advisor and virtual filmmaker produced a virtual videotape of a family in a Syrian refugee camp.[11] After showing the film to stakeholders in the UN, Arora reported the dramatic difference this made even in viewers already familiar with the situation. He reported that seeing a situation with which they believed they were already familiar as a virtual reality, a reality they "participated" in rather than viewed statically, brought them to tears. There was a new depth of empathy as the viewers literally entered into and became immersed in virtual relationship with the camp environment and the refugees.

We believe that this depth of empathy and visceral understanding, though perhaps not as accessible as it once was, remains available to us even without virtual technology. It is the same empathy and understanding we have for someone we have come to truly know, with whom we have, as the old American Indian saying puts it, "walked in their shoes." If Choosing Relationship over Control can help us achieve that, it will have met its purpose as a facilitator of respectful, reciprocal and responsive communication and collaboration. Any movement toward relationship in this sense, however, will support respectful, reciprocal and responsive communication and collaboration.

Setting the Stage for Miracles

The disposition of Setting the Stage for Miracles builds on and extends the disposition of Choosing Relationship Over Control by focusing on the power of paradox. It involves being disposed not only to enter into a relational interaction with another individual but to do so knowing that his or her perspectives no matter how diverse or seemingly contradictory, may in fact be complementary with our own. It is with this premise that Setting the Stage for Miracles invites us to step outside of what we believe should or must happen and become open to happenings and outcomes that cannot be predicted given prior data (i.e., "miracles").

The relationship between Choosing Relationship over Control and Setting the Stage for Miracles is a reciprocal one. On the one hand, without Setting the Stage for miracles, Choosing Relationship over Control cannot be sustained. Outside of relationship aspects of control will remain and inhibit our ability to see, much less develop, ways of leveraging the complementarity of differences. On the other hand, without Choosing Relationship over Control, the potential synergy that can be generated by differences remains untapped.

Without Setting the Stage for Miracles, the uncertainty and unpredictability that are natural consequences of choosing relationship over control will remain merely uncertainty and unpredictability that prompt us to shift into control. When approached with the disposition of Setting the Stage for Miracles, however, uncertainty and unpredictability become a springboard to "breakthrough thinking" (Perkins, 2000), which can take us beyond stalemates of familiar either-or understandings and interpretations of differences.

Being disposed to set the stage for miracles promotes the creation of conceptual and interactional space within which two or more diverse realities (i.e., beliefs, perspectives, behaviors) can be integrated without needing to blur or erase the differences between them. Skilled Dialogue refers to this space as *3rd Space*, a paradoxical space where both contradiction and complementarity are simultaneously true. This concept of 3rd Space can be visually depicted by the yin/yang symbol common in Asian cultures, where it is a much more familiar concept than in Western cultures (see illustration in Part III).

More specifically, the following characteristics are true of 3rd Space as defined within Skilled Dialogue:

(1) diverse perspectives and beliefs are understood to be distinct as well as complementary; each is understood to reflect some aspect of the other to a greater or lesser degree,

(2) there is no need for forced either-or choices between perspectives or beliefs; i.e., the choice of one does not necessitate the rejection or rebuttal of another, and finally,

(3) the "whole" created by the integration of differences is composed of both existing perspectives yet is more than either side by side. It is more than the sum of its parts

Because 3rd Space is neither a simple concept nor one familiar to many people in the U.S., additional information and exercises for understanding and creating it are provided in Part III. For now, we will merely say that it is the essential underpinning of this disposition.

Without the disposition of Setting the Stage for Miracles we can all too easily find ourselves boxed in by familiar divisions and polarities, pushing to reduce or eliminate one thing in order to actualize a second. One way to understand the disposition of Setting the Stage for Miracles, then, is to think of it as being willing to remain grounded in the differences between existing perspectives and beliefs while *simultaneously* allowing for the possibility of a common reality inclusive of those differences.

Choosing Relationship Over Control thus needs Setting the Stage for Miracles to actualize its full potential in reference to communication and collaboration. While Choosing Relationship Over Control leads to the recognition of the legitimacy of another's diverse perspective, it still leaves diverse perspectives separate—contradictory at worst, side-by-side at best—frozen with an either-this-or-that frame that explicitly or implicitly privileges one perspective over another. Only when Setting the Stage for Miracles is added to Choosing Relationship Over Control can diverse views be leveraged so as to allow their individual strengths to work together rather than against each other.

The disposition of Setting the Stage for Miracles drives the co-construction of inclusive options that unite "this way" (i.e., mine) and "that way" (i.e., yours) while continuing to honor the uniqueness of each. Seeking to co-construct options does not, however, mean that one person's familiar or favored perspective or belief is never chosen over another's. It simply means that surrender or compromise of one perspective in favor of another is neither forced nor a prerequisite to continuing communication and collaboration.

The arena of bilingual education, a topic that often produces fierce antagonism between those who advocate English only and those that advocate the maintenance of a language other than English, provides a relatively simple example of Setting the Stage for Miracles. Adopting this disposition shifts the focus from this language or that language to the underlying reality of linguistic competence, the larger 3rd Space within which both English proficiency and Spanish (or other language) proficiency exist. It invites us to seek a person's current linguistic strengths (e.g., reads, tells stories, is highly verbal) in whatever language that person uses to enhance and expedite the use of both languages. This is, in fact, what research into language development reveals: that eliminating one language is not a prerequisite for linguistic competence in another; that it can, in fact, actually slow or impede the development of a second language. It is the continued use of one language rather than its discontinuation that supports the development of a second language.

At this point it may be helpful to revisit the characteristics of 3rd Space:

(1) Reality in 3rd Space is non-dichotomous; that is, it is perceived on a spectrum where one choice is not exclusive of the other (e.g., a rainbow's colors) rather than on a continuum where reaching one end means leaving the other.

(2) 3rd Space requires generating creative alternatives beyond the obvious; that is, it requires understanding that there are always more than two either-or views of reality.

(3) Differences are understood to be complementary rather than divisive; i.e., two or more perspectives no matter how seemingly contradictory can be integrated into a larger whole.

(4) The borders that define different perspectives and beliefs are understood to serve both as distinctions and as points of

contact that, like the poles of a battery, generate constructive tension when connected.

(5) The sum of two or more differences is always more than just the differences side-by-side; i.e., the whole is greater than the sum of the parts

An example of creating 3rd Space that comes from Southwest Airlines is referenced in one of our earlier books. Faced with two strong yet diverse customer perspectives—one that advocated assigned seating so that customers didn't need to stand in line in order to ensure preferred sitting, and one that vastly preferred open sitting no matter what it took to get it, Southwest generated an alternative that went beyond the obvious. They started to assign numbered boarding passes (e.g., A1, A2, and so on) that defined passengers' places in line but left seating choices open. These removed any need to stand in place until just before boarding yet allowed passengers to choose seating once boarded. Both original views were honored without placing them on an exclusive either-or continuum that required eliminating one to achieve the other. In effect they created a 3rd Space option where both views became complementary and could be simultaneously honored.

While examples of 3rd Space such as this can be given, 3rd Space is not a space that can be pre-identified. The stage can be set for it to emerge but it cannot be pre-identified. To pre-identify it outside of an interactive context negates its intent: to stimulate unexpected and/or unanticipated synergy between diverse perspectives and beliefs.

Even when a person has worked with this disposition for a long time and can, from past experience, envision how it might work in a particular interaction, it remains important that such envisioning not be frozen into expectations or that it not be perceived by other(s) as directive or imposed rather than co-constructed. As my first boss once said, there are times when even suggestions carry the implicit message: "This is only a suggestion *but don't forget who made it.*" Anything that unbalances relationship and reciprocity works contrary to Setting the Stage for Miracles.

Both Setting the Stage for Miracles and Choosing Relationship over Control find their concrete expressions in the Skilled Dialogue strategies discussed in the following chapters.

Discussion Questions/Activities

1. How do you understand the disposition of Choosing Relationship over Control? Discuss your understanding of the following paragraph:

   "Control, as used in the title of this disposition, refers not just to controlling other's actions or choices. It also refers to control of other aspects of communicative interactions such as control of knowledge (e.g., this knowledge should prevail over that knowledge because it's truer or better), control of situations (e.g., things must happen or be done this way and only this way in order to meet X goal), and control of time (e.g., appointment times that are non-negotiable, unilaterally set agendas). While these aspects of control are often subtle and unconscious, their power to disrupt relationship (i.e., sabotage the power of the other) is as strong if not stronger than that of more explicit forms of control."

2. Have you ever had interactions in which you've felt as a generic category rather than as an individual or felt controlled? In what situations has this been true? Contrast these with situations when you have felt truly "seen" as a unique person with value? What was the difference between these interactions?

3. What is your understanding of Setting the Stage for Miracles and of how paradox sets the stage for "miracles"?
   What needs to be in place for "miracles" to occur?

4. Discuss the disposition of Setting the Stage for Miracles with others and identify at least three examples of a paradox that reflects it.

5. Think of a recent interaction with someone whose views or perspectives were significantly different from your own in which you wanted something to happen that was not currently happening or wanted something that was happening to stop

happening. Describe your desired outcome as clearly and specifically as you can.

Now think of all the obstacles to that outcome that immediately come to mind. List those; they may be about you (e.g., "I don't know how to do that") or about the other (e.g., "They would never do that"). Again, describe them as clearly as you can without censoring them or telling yourself you shouldn't believe that. NOW, hold both desired outcome and obstacles in your mind at the same time, side by side. Reflect on your experience as you do that. Were you able to do it? Did one seem more real than the other? Were you able to allow the energy between the two to simply be? If you could, what happened then?

6. An example of Setting the Stage for Miracles is given in this chapter in relation to bilingual education. An action taken by Southwest Airlines is also given as an example. What do you think about this example? Are you familiar with any other examples? Brainstorm with other people to identify additional examples of 3rd Space.

Chapter 5

Honoring Identity through the Strategies of Welcoming and Allowing

"the first opportunity to shift the quality of conversation…often arises when people area confronted with an opinion with which they disagree and find they must choose whether or not to defend their views."
(Senge, Scharmer, Jaworski & Flowers, 2004).

(NOTE: This chapter initiates a general discussion of the individual Skilled Dialogue strategies. Additional information along with examples and non-examples is contained in Chapter 9. It may be useful to read that chapter in conjunction with this chapter.)

Skilled Dialogue's first two strategies, *Welcoming* and *Allowing*[12], focus on establishing a respectful context for communication and collaboration through honoring identity. They are designed to set a base for acknowledging and accessing diverse strengths and resources without negating or diminishing differences. In doing this, they model the respect we wish others to demonstrate in return.

Welcoming and *Allowing* explicitly honor another's identity, not necessarily because we admire them or even agree with them, but *because they, like us, are negotiating their lives as best they can based on their experiential data*. Both strategies involve communicating the legitimacy of others' behaviors and beliefs as evidence-based even when they may not be the best choices within given contexts.

Honoring another's identity through these strategies is not, however, intended to deny either the consequences of someone's behavior or the value to that person of alternative behaviors. Certain behaviors can and do result in life-threatening conditions for those holding them as well as for others. Honoring identity through these strategies is intended to affirm the humanity of those exhibiting those behaviors accords and not the goodness or efficacy of behaviors that diminish resources or life.

Welcoming and *Allowing* explicitly communicate recognition of the legitimacy of diverse behaviors and perspectives as evidence-based expressions of identity. They set a non-judgmental context without which neither communication nor collaboration efforts can fully succeed. A lack of these strategies communicates, however unintentionally, a kind of interpersonal violence in "the imposition of [one person's] point of view [on another] with little or no understanding [of that other]" (Isaacs, p. 132).

More specifically, *Welcoming* initiates the disposition of Choosing Relationship Over Control while *Allowing* initiates Setting the Stage for Miracles. The table below illustrates this relationship between these strategies and the dispositions and qualities associated with each.

DISPOSITIONS

QUALITY	Choosing Relationship over Control	Setting the Stage for Miracles
	Welcoming	*Allowing:*
RESPECT *Honoring Identity THRU Explicit Acknowledgment of Boundaries*	Hallmark: Positive regard of other Critical Question: Am I looking forward to this interaction confident I'll learn something new?	Hallmark: Expression of other's perspective w/o contradictory remarks or defense of mine Critical Question: Can I listen to other without needing to defend my views?

Welcoming

At first glance *Welcoming* seems to be the simplest of Skilled Dialogue's strategies. Its purpose is simple: to welcome another regardless of how different his or her viewpoint may be from ours. What makes it not so simple is its deeper purpose: to communicate the recognition of that other as being capable and meriting dignity, not because of how they believe or act as we do but because they are human like us. It is this deeper purpose that makes *Welcoming* an essential strategy for establishing a tone of respect for subsequent interactions. As such, it has two dimensions: welcoming the person(s) with whom we are interacting, (e.g., "I'm glad you're here; I'm glad to be meeting you), and welcoming the opportunity they offer to learn and grow. The latter aspect seeks to communicate that the interaction is more than merely a means to an end (i.e., that it is relational rather than merely tactical).

Welcoming the person. There is a subtle yet discernible difference in nonverbal behavior (and, sometimes, in verbal) behavior when we meet someone we perceive to be as capable as ourselves and when we meet someone we perceive as less capable than ourselves in some way. The people we interact with will, typically, feel welcomed when the former is true and disrespected or somehow not welcomed when the former is true. A key aspect of *Welcoming* is, thus, communicating our acknowledgement of the other as someone whose perspectives, beliefs, and/or behaviors are as competent in relation to the context(s) in which they were learned as ours are in relation to the contexts in which we learned them. *Welcoming* thus communicates that we see the person we are interacting with as someone whose perspectives, beliefs and behaviors are the result of competent adaptation to a specific context and have positive value no matter how maladaptive or "wrong" they may seem or actually be outside that context. (See endnote # 5 and related discussion in Chapter 1)

Explicit statements and concrete behaviors that communicate *Welcoming* are important. These can include general welcoming statements spoken sincerely (e.g., "I'm glad you're here." "I'm looking forward to talking/working with you." "Thank you for making the time to meet with me." "Do you have any questions before we start?"). *Welcoming* can also include more specific responses related to a person's concerns or expressed emotions. After exchanging greetings, for example, a person may express their displeasure with having to meet or work with you. At that point, *Welcoming* can involve statements such as the following: "Can you tell me more about that?" "I'm so sorry to hear that. Can you tell me a bit more?" or "I'm sorry to hear that, would you like to reschedule our meeting?"

Nonverbal welcoming behaviors that support verbal expressions are equally important expressions of *Welcoming*. These behaviors can, for example, include the use of relaxed body language, positive facial expressions and maintaining a culturally appropriate distance from the other person. They should also include giving our full attention to another as we are interacting with them (e.g., not checking the time or answering our cell phone). *Welcoming* may at times be expressed more subtly through less direct responses that are more general and do not explicitly address what the other has said (e.g., I see; Hm-m; I hadn't thought of that; head nods.). These communicate our willingness to create a space for listening.

How *Welcoming* is expressed depends on both the context within which a given interaction is taking place (e.g., in a business, in a home) and on the preferred social and cultural patterns of the people involved. For that reason, *Welcoming* can involve behaviors that may appear irrelevant or off task (e.g., asking about family or about the other's day) yet are essential aspects of welcoming in some cultures and social settings.

It is important to distinguish responses that communicate a lack of *Welcoming* from responses that are truly welcoming. When, for example, one person says "I'm not really sure why we're having this meeting," there is a difference between responses like "I'm so glad you're here" or "We're here to talk about X," and responses like "Oh, can you say a bit more about that?" or "Would you like more information or do you have other questions about this meeting?" The former, which may be called parallel responses, shift the focus from the speaker to the person holding the meeting. They indicate not only a lack of welcoming but also a lack of attention to the speaker. In so doing they make it clear that the speaker is not really being heard much less welcomed.

Similarly, one person may say "I really feel we need to attend to X" and another person may respond by saying "We've just had so much to do lately." When this happens there is a significant likelihood that the first person will not feel welcomed. While there may indeed be a lot to do and while that may be the reason X has not been attended to, this statement like the earlier ones shifts the focus from the person with the concern to the person to whom the concern was brought. It does not communicate that either the person or the level of concern expressed is welcomed. A more welcoming response might be "I can hear how much that matters to you" or "I can see how concerned you are about that" followed by "Can you tell me more?" or even "I really want to hear more about this issue. Can you give me a bit of time to set up a meeting to discuss it more fully?"

Welcoming responses neither switch the topic nor devalue a person's expressed concern by delaying attention to it or explaining it away (e.g., I know you're concerned about X but actually there's nothing to be concerned about. X actually happens quite often; It happens because....). However it is communicated, a lack of *Welcoming* always leaves at least one person deeply dissatisfied and less willing to accord credibility or respect to the other.

Ultimately, *Welcoming* is determined by the person(s) with whom we are interacting rather than by our intention or words. Even when we intend to be welcoming, if we are not perceived to be so, communication and collaboration will be negatively affected. It is, thus, important to be attentive to any signs of discomfort or un-welcome from the person(s) with whom we are interacting. If these are detected, *Welcoming* can also encompass explicit statements such as "I'm wondering if you're feeling comfortable with our discussion." "Is there anything I can do to help you feel more welcome?" or, even more directly, "Am I saying or doing anything that you're not comfortable with?"

Welcoming, like all of the Skilled Dialogue strategies, cannot be scripted ahead of time. For that reason, focusing on its disposition— Choosing Relationship over Control—is critically important. That focus can help to keep us aligned with the goal of *Welcoming*: to model the receptivity to the relationship we wish to engender in the person(s) with whom we are interacting. (see also Chapter 9.)

Welcoming the opportunity another offers us to learn and grow. As used in Skilled Dialogue *Welcoming* encompasses welcoming another as well as welcoming the opportunity to learn and grow offered by that other's diverse perspectives, beliefs, and behaviors (i.e., perceiving these as sources of potential and mutually beneficial riches both to us individually and to desired collaboration). It is always useful when engaging in communication and collaboration with a particular goal in mind to realize that encountering another's diverse perspectives, beliefs, and behaviors can provide us, at least potentially, with an increased awareness of previously unimagined alternatives. There is, after all, always more than one way to reach a goal as well as to realize that that goal may not be the only one available to us.

This aspect of *Welcoming* focuses on communicating our interest in learning about and from the other. Behaviors such as, for example, staying relaxed when hearing what someone has to tell us even when we disagree can be helpful in this regard. Another way to communicate our interest in what another can offer is through how we set our interactional space. When this space is set, for example, with a large desk and a chair in front of it, the message is clearly that information will flow one way, "from the desk to the chair." A friend once told me of an occasion when she was meeting with the parents of a child she was teaching. The room where the meeting was being held contained one large easy chair and several comfortable but smaller chairs. When the parents came in she stood up and pointed to the easy chair, indicating that was were one of them was to sit. She remained standing until they both sat down, clearly communicating not only that their comfort was important but that she valued their presence as partners in the meeting. (Note: Cultural differences can play a critical role in the language and behaviors that express *Welcoming*. Readers can find additional information on taking these differences into account in our previous books.)

Assessment Questions. Questions such as the following can help to assess the presence or absence of *Welcoming*:

Do I perceive the individual(s) with whom I seek to communicate or collaborate positively or negatively? (Even when nothing is said, others can often pick up on our perceptions.)

Am I assuming that I know better or more, or that the others' time is less important than mine? (The likelihood is that if I am, then, no matter my behavior, welcoming will be absent, however subtly or unintentionally.)

A related question that goes a bit deeper is "What assumptions about the other underlie my interactions with them?" Am I basing these assumptions solely or primarily on inferences and interpretations rather than seeking a concrete evidence base? If I am, I undermine the purpose of *Welcoming* to honor who someone is (i.e., their identity) rather than who I believe them to be. The importance of this distinction was strongly emphasized for me (Barrera) through an early experience as a university professor before Skilled Dialogue was conceptualized as it is now. In teaching a class on the challenges of cultural diversity I talked about the impact of appearances. In doing so, I made reference to data indicating that tall White males tend to be promoted and receive higher salaries in corporate settings. There was a tall white male in the class who later emailed me telling me how upset he'd been during the class and how wrong I'd been in placing him in that category when I asked if he'd had that experience. He told me that he been largely raised by his best friend's family, who was Black, in a dominantly Hispanic neighborhood where his own family was one of the few White families. I apologized sincerely to him and have never forgotten that lesson.[13]

Needless to say, he had not felt welcomed in my class that day. Without knowing it I had dishonored his identity, ironically by pointing out strengths I believed it had yet missing who he really was. I had, without thinking, acted on inferences based on external characteristics and my own suppositions.

This example carries us into a third question that can assess the presence of absence of *Welcoming*: "Is what I assume about the person with whom I am interacting absolutely and unequivocally true?"[14] In the example above, it was obvious that the answer would have been "No." The purpose of this question is to soften our reliance on our assumptions as unquestionably true. This softening is necessary to open us up to the possibility that others' perspectives and beliefs, even when apparently contradictory to our own, are as valid as our own.

Finally, there is a fourth question: "Have I exhibited specific behaviors that express a willingness to welcome perspectives and beliefs that differ from those I hold?" Though not necessarily specific to particular interactions these behaviors, when observed by others, can affect those interactions.

These questions serve to assess the presence or absence of *Welcoming* as well as of the disposition toward Choosing Relationship Over Control that underlies this strategy. They also serve to guide to building a respectful base for optimum communication and collaboration. (See Chapter 9 for further discussion of *Welcoming*.)

Allowing

Skilled Dialogue not only promotes relationship be chosen over control; it also promotes setting the stage for miracles. *Welcoming* addresses the first; *Allowing*, the second.

Allowing extends and reinforces *Welcoming* by making time for the explicit expression of another's identity without interrupting, discounting or devaluing what is said as well as without the need for explanations or defense of our own perspective, either silently in our heads or aloud in words.

Like *Welcoming*, *Allowing* seems deceptively simple: listen without interruption. Our experience as we trained others in Skilled Dialogue, however, revealed it as one of the more difficult strategies to learn. Even in simulated training scenarios where the differences were hypothetical, participants regularly found it difficult to simply listen without interruption to perspectives different from their own. This was especially true when they were in the role of a person with status or power (e.g., a teacher or supervisor) interacting with someone they were supervising, directing or otherwise seeking to help (e.g., a student, a supervisee). They tended to get caught up in the role they were playing and the behaviors associated with that role rather than in the actual interaction that was occurring.

Allowing is both about listening and, most importantly, about what uninterrupted listening communicates: the validation of another's perspectives or beliefs as legitimate and evidence based. We welcomed these perspectives with *Welcoming*, now this second strategy is about allowing their expression explicitly as well as implicitly.

In the previous example of my interaction with a student in one of my classes I had not explicitly disallowed the expression of his identity. Nevertheless, by boxing it into a single description alien to him, I had in effect not allowed him to express it. Consequently, I could neither realize nor access his strengths.

Allowing creates a context within which the strengths within another's identity can unfold as that identity is expressed. It does not necessitate or mean that my own perspectives or beliefs are any less valid or that I will change my mind about the need for change. It does encourage an open mind about the possibility of such change as well as of how such change might happen.

Three distinct characteristics are associated with *Allowing*. The first of these is a willingness to stay with the tension of differing perspectives or values without seeking to diminish or dissolve it by choosing one over the other. Our willingness to refrain from resolving the incompatibilities that generate that tension explicitly communicates our respect for another's diverse perspective or values.

Allowing involves refraining from putting contradictory perspectives and beliefs into rigid judgment-based either-or dichotomies. For example, *Allowing* supports believing that though a person's behavior seems to reflect a lack of caring according to our data, it may in fact, reflect that they care in ways we cannot conceive, however unskilled those ways might be. *Allowing* is not, however, about permitting behaviors that violate legal or personal boundaries (e.g., are abusive or illegal). While it is important to suspend judgment of the other as "bad" or uncaring or deficient, it is equally important in all situations to take appropriate action to curtail inappropriate behavior (e.g., call protective services).

A second characteristic of *Allowing* follows from this nonjudgmental stance: the release of the "stories" we tell ourselves about another's identity and about what their behaviors mean. As put by Stone, Patton & Heen (1999):

Difficult conversations that sabotage communication and collaboration most often happen when parts of our story collide with important parts of someone else's story. When this happens, we blame how *they* are or what they believe. Actually, the dissonance and disagreement is the result of our stories merely being different (not contradictory) and our believing that one is more true or valid than the other or that only one can be true or valid at all!

Releasing our stories requires acknowledging that they reflect our experience and knowledge base rather than undeniable fact. We may, for example, believe that someone who is from a particular cultural, social group or economic class has particular characteristics, ignoring the many people from those same groups with different characteristics. Or we may believe that someone who is consistently late is also irresponsible without seeking other explanations.

Our stories about others' perspectives, beliefs and behaviors are only our explanations and interpretations of another's behaviors, perhaps true, perhaps not. When we disallow other explanations and interpretations, we remain tied to only our own stories, limiting the expression of others' identities as they really are. We also consequently lost the opportunity to identify and leverage the strengths of the differences in those identities.

Releasing our natural inclination to focus on solutions and resolutions is a third characteristic of *Allowing*. It is one that can make the ones just discussed a little easier to practice. There are, of course, times when time may be of the essence. In most cases, however, it is our discomfort rather than a time limit that drives us to push for resolution. When discussions are not allowed to unfold organically, we sabotage the very relationship we are seeking to establish. We communicate, however unintentionally, that we neither respect the person with whom we are interacting nor trust that they can contribute meaningfully to the solution or resolution we seek.

Ultimately, the clearest behavioral evidence of *Allowing* is behavior such as the following: (a) the allowance of "voice time" for another to express their diverse perspectives, (b) refraining from using "buts" and other similar words, and (c) not interrupting except for clarification of what the other has said. These behaviors communicate openness to another's beliefs, perspectives, or opinions without sacrificing adherence to our own beliefs, perspectives, and opinions.

The importance of *Allowing* lies in explicitly permitting differences to stand without minimizing or eliminating them in order to "set the stage" for the integration of diverse perspectives addressed in subsequent strategies.

<u>Assessment Questions</u>. Questions such as the following can be used to assess the degree to which *Allowing* is in place:

"Am I allowing the person(s) with whom I am interacting to state their own ideas/concerns without interruption other than to ask for clarification if necessary?"

"Am I making room for the other's perceptions and beliefs and not just asking that they understand mine?

"If I don't agree with the other(s), am I staying with that tension without trying to minimize or remove it, or am I pushing to resolve it?" That is, "Am I willing to simply listen even when I don't agree or don't see the value of what the other is saying?"

"Am I really listening and not just giving the other(s) time so that I get their cooperation or plan my rebuttal?

"Am I sharing rather than imposing my stories and what I think should be on those with whom I interact?"

"Am I willing to acknowledge that my explanations and interpretations of others' behaviors are only <u>stories</u>, mental constructions based on my own experiential data and sociocultural contexts, and, therefore, are not necessarily true?"

For *Allowing* to achieve its intended goal it needs to be clear that I am willing to truly listen without interruption and learn from views other than my own. As stated earlier, this doesn't necessarily mean that I approve of those views or that I desire them to remain unchanged. It does mean that I'm willing to perceive diverse views as legitimate given the data pool on which they are based, and that I'll remain open to learn more about them with the conviction that they may somehow add something of value to a given situation.

Discussion Questions/Activities

1. Think back over interactions you've had with others. Do you tend to interrupt or defend your viewpoint rather than simply listening when their opinions differ from yours?

2. What do you think the authors mean by the statement: *There is a subtle difference in nonverbal behavior and, sometimes, in verbal behavior as well, when we express welcoming to someone we believe is as capable as ourselves as compared to someone we believe is less capable in some way.*

3. Why is it critical to explicitly permit differences to stand without minimizing or eliminating them?

4. What do you see as your personal challenge(s) in implementing the strategies of *Welcoming* and *Allowing?*

Describe the challenge(s) and what you might do to address them.

Chapter 6

Establishing Reciprocity through Sense-making and Appreciating

"Dialogue is not about trying to change anyone's opinions but is about understanding that people's opinions, their truths, can actually be a contribution to a collective truth. That is perhaps the fundamental purpose of dialogue—to create a shared understanding beyond our individual points of view." (Zaiss, 2002)

This chapter continues the general discussion of Skilled Dialogue strategies by focusing on *Sense-making* and *Appreciating*, which simultaneously build on and facilitate *Welcoming* and *Allowing*. These strategies are designed to establish reciprocity.

The importance of reciprocity relative to communication and collaboration cannot be understated. Not only is it essential to building and sustaining respect, it is also critical to the understanding of another's statements. Even in relatively simple communication that appears to be straightforward (e.g., giving directions or following instructions), the shortcomings of one-way (i.e., non-reciprocal) communication are amply evident (e.g., GPS devices and smart phone features such as Siri[©].

Gernsbacher's (2006) words on reciprocity, written about interactions with children and adults with autism, are no less true for interactions with anyone whose understanding of the world differs from our own. She tells of a child with autism, who when asked what she would wish for if she had a magic wand, responds that she "wished others could see the world through her eyes" (p. 141). That phrase—to see the world through another's eyes—captures the essence of reciprocity as addressed by both *Sense-Making* and *Appreciating*. To dialogue skillfully with others it is not enough to simply respect them (i.e., welcome them and allow for the expression of their identity). It is also critical to make sense of and appreciate how they see the world. Only then can we enter into interactions that are two-way rather than one-way.

Sense-Making and *Appreciating* are designed to increase awareness of others' perspectives, beliefs and behaviors in ways that allow us to tap into and leverage the strengths of those perspectives, beliefs and behaviors vis-à-vis our own. *Sense-Making* seeks to first figure out how others' perspectives and behaviors make sense. *Appreciating* then focuses on exploring ways of appreciating those perspectives and behaviors as something of value. Together, these strategies unleash the synergy of diverse strengths for generating optimum communication and collaboration.

There are, however, situations in which reciprocity cannot be established or is inappropriate. For that reason, *Sense-Making* and *Appreciating* need to be clearly understood before attempting to apply them. These strategies are NEVER intended to minimize or ignore the seriousness of potential or actual harmful behaviors or beliefs. They should not be attempted in cases where they might be misunderstood as accepting such behaviors or beliefs. Nor should they be attempted in situations where one person's openness to another's behaviors or beliefs can be used to control or overpower that person. It is necessary that the identity of <u>all</u> those in an interaction be honored before seeking to establish reciprocity (see earlier footnote in Chapter 1). Just how *Sense-Making* and *Appreciating* apply in those situations is addressed below as each is described in more detail.

Sense-Making

Understanding anything requires first understanding the context within which it sits. *Sense-Making* challenges us to do just this, to become curious about how other's perspectives, beliefs, and behaviors make sense in the context(s) in which they have developed so that we can affirm that, even when we do not like or value those perspectives, beliefs or behaviors, we can nevertheless communicate our understanding that they (a) make sense based on the experience and socio-cultural context of the person who has them (i.e., that they are not choosing it out of ignorance or willful self destruction) and (b) are perspectives or behaviors with which we can relate to some degree. The latter is something often overlooked. Yet, when someone's perspective or behavior does not make sense to us—or we can only relate to it negatively, interactions remain one-sided, side-by-side monologues, with neither "side" reciprocating the other's perspectives or concerns.

Sense-Making thus focuses on first respectfully gathering contextual data for identifying how someone else's perspectives, beliefs or behaviors make sense to them and then identifying how they might mirror our own perspectives, beliefs or behaviors to at least some degree. The latter is important if we are to truly make sense of another's perspectives, beliefs or behaviors. It shifts our interpretation of those from "That makes absolutely no sense" to "Ah, I can see how that, or something very much like that, makes sense (because I can see myself holding similar perspectives and beliefs, or acting in similar ways)."

Sense-Making does not deny how dysfunctional, unskilled or life-denying some perspectives, beliefs, or behaviors can be outside of or even within their given contexts. Instead, it seeks to answer why, in a particular context, those perspectives, beliefs, and behaviors are believed to be better than the alternatives, even when their dysfunctional or life-denying aspects are recognized. Vigorous disagreeing or even fighting might, for example, make sense to someone if the alternative is perceived to be leaving oneself open to violation—and experience in one's context has shown that to be so. In this instance behaviors such as verbal abuse would be associated with protecting boundaries and thus "make sense." Though we might not exhibit them ourselves or not exhibit them to the degree as the person using them "against" us, we could then understand their validity in their context. The latter is an important aspect of *Sense-Making*. If we cannot imagine ourselves exhibiting some aspect of another's behavior, it is challenging if not impossible to truly make sense of it. It remains non-sensible, foreign or unimaginable.

A second example might be not going for medical check-ups. This behavior might, "make sense" for an individual if he or she had a strong fear of what might be learned and believed they would be helpless to remedy a consequent negative outcome. Here again, it is the second half of the statement that is important. It "makes sense" to omit a medical check-up if we believe—and have data from our particular context—that there is nothing we can do about a negative outcome to a medical check-up. Implementing *Sense-Making* would invite us to ask when we, too, have avoided a situation out of fear of what might result.

Making sense of behaviors or beliefs we cannot understand or find negative can be difficult. It is often necessary to see beyond exaggerated expressions to their positive intent and to catch glimpses of similar behaviors or beliefs in our selves, though perhaps in a much more muted form. Making sense of another's beliefs and behaviors in this fashion permits us to give others equal voice when interacting with them. Without equal voice it becomes all too easy to believe and communicate, however inadvertently or unintentionally, that the person with whom we seek to communicate and collaborate has nothing of value or relevance to contribute. This ultimately sabotages respect, no matter how skillfully we thought we'd established it through *Welcoming* and *Allowing*.

There are two critical aspects of *Sense-Making*. The first invites us to become curious enough to ask "I wonder how this makes sense." Thus, instead of coming from a place of "This obviously means X," or "This makes absolutely no sense," *Sense-Making* prompts us to ask questions such as the following:

"Why does this person believe that their belief, behavior, or perspective is more appropriate than other beliefs, behaviors, perspectives (like mine)?"

"What understanding of how the world works underlies this person's chosen beliefs, behaviors or perspectives?"

"What do they believe would happen if they did not hold that perspective or express that behavior?"

Rather than relying on familiar interpretations and "stories" to interpret diverse perspectives, *Sense-Making* invites us to approach interactions with a beginner's or learner's mind free from the blindness of certainty (Langer, 2005). Without a learner's mind our perceptions of and responses to diverse perspectives remain fixed, keeping those who hold them equally fixed in the role of receivers with nothing to contribute except their acquiescence.

Sense-Making also invites us to shift our perspective from a judgmental, nonreciprocal stance (e.g., "I'd never choose that behavior or hold that perspective") to a reciprocal stance (e.g., "What can I learn from that behavior or perspective?" "What would it take for me to choose that same behavior or hold that same perspective?"). Statements such as "Tell me more" or "I see" can be simple tools for gathering data that can lead to a reciprocal stance. More specific examples and non-examples of *Sense-Making* can be found in Chapter 9.

Assessment questions. Several questions are useful in determining if we are authentically communicating the intent to make sense of another's diverse perspectives and behaviors.

"To what degree am I interested in learning how the other understands and feels about the current situation/problem?" When such interest is genuinely present, it is much more likely that our behaviors will reflect it.

"Can I honestly say that perspective or behavior makes sense? If not, what additional information might I need?" If there is sufficient rapport already established, it might be appropriate to say something like "I'm not sure how this makes sense. My experiences have been quite different but I'd really like to know why/how you see it as your best choice at this time. Would you be willing to tell me?" or "I'm thinking that you don't see what I'm describing/asking as positive from your perspective. Would you tell me what it would mean to you (or what you think would happen) if you did/believed X instead of Y (what you're doing/believing now)?" While the specific words used would, of course, need to be adapted to particular contexts, the idea is to communicate an honest desire to understand, not to agree or disagree.

Can I honestly say "Ah, now I understand. I think I'd do the same or something similar if I were in your shoes" or maybe even "I've done something similar though not as consistently or to the same degree." This question is, perhaps, the one that most find truly challenging. It can also be stated differently: Can I believe that, given the same life experiences and situations, I'd make the same choices and/or behave in the same or similar ways?" Making sense to this degree is key to Skilled Dialogue's next strategy.

Appreciating

Skilled Dialogue uses the word "appreciating" in the sense of being fully aware of or sensitive to, as in "I appreciate your concern and understand why you believe it needs immediate attention." More specifically, *Appreciating* is about explicitly acknowledging the validity and value of another's behaviors, beliefs, or perspectives. It involves identifying the value that other's unique contributions bring to a particular interaction or situation.

Appreciating seeks to establish the reciprocity necessary for successful collaboration. In this fashion it models learning from another and consequently stimulates others' willingness to learn from us. A critical aspect of *Appreciating*, therefore, is to identify what is of value in another's diverse perspective; i.e., to identify positive kernels or "gold nuggets." Rosinki's comment in reference to cultural differences is equally applicable in reference to all differences: "Leveraging cultural differences is a proactive attitude. You look for gems [i.e., nuggets of gold] in your own culture(s) and mine for treasures in other culture(s). ...The riches appear in the form of useful insights, [and] alternative perspectives on issues...." (p. 40).

While it is relatively simple to identify the value of perspectives we deem to be positive, (e.g. timeliness) it can be challenging to do so with perspectives we deem negative (e.g., tardiness). A useful skill in learning to appreciate these latter perspectives, is to reframe them as exaggerated or misdirected versions of positive perspectives. For example, tardiness might be more about exaggerated attention to a person or task in front of us than about disrespect for a task not yet begun or a person not yet before us. In this sense, it is, thus, actually the result of misdirected respect.

Reframing in this fashion involves breaking open the familiar ways we typically perceive and understand particular perspectives, behaviors, and beliefs to allow for alternative perceptions and understandings. Our familiar perceptual and interpretative frames stem from assumptions we hold that lock in a particular view or understanding (e.g., I cannot appreciate tardiness because it reflects a lack of respect). Chapter 8 contains further information on and examples of re-framing.

Ultimately, *Appreciating* invites the person(s) with whom we interact to work with us reciprocally, as partners with something of value to offer rather than only as receivers of what we bring to the interaction. Part III provides concrete examples to further clarify *Appreciating*.

Assessment questions. Several questions can help assess the degree to which we are appreciating another's diverse beliefs, behaviors or perspectives. These include questions such as "What can I learn from the diverse perspectives, beliefs, and behaviors held by the person with whom I am interacting?" In the face of someone who believes in keeping precise track of things perhaps I could learn to recognize the importance of organization, or, of disorganization, if I am the one who prizes organization.

A second related question is: "What about the other's behaviors/ beliefs mirrors something I am lacking or not appreciating in myself?" Answering this question invites recognition of another's diversity as a mirror of what I myself may need. If I am very organized, for example, appreciating the value of disorganization can keep me from becoming overly rigid or obsessed with order.

Finally, "What is positive, though perhaps exaggerated, about another's behaviors and beliefs?" is a third similar question. Some degree of disorganization can, for example, be a positive contribution to creativity. When it is exaggerated to the degree that order is completely lost or neglected, however, disorganization blocks rather than supports creativity. *Appreciating* thus may involve dialing down the intensity of the diverse perspectives, beliefs, and/or behaviors we find so troublesome.

These questions and our answers to them must be genuine. Sometimes Skilled Dialogue workshop participants have given answers such as "I appreciate his behavior because I learned how not to do things like he does." While that may in fact reflect learning, it is not learning that can easily lead to genuine communication and collaboration. Sometimes, we hear "I learned that I never want to do that!" That also is a real learning, yet one that negates *Appreciating*. Genuine appreciation is reflected in statements such as the following "Wow, that person really taught me something of value" or "Wow, that person really taught me something about myself." Until appreciation is genuinely present, interactions remain unbalanced by a lack of reciprocity, sabotaging the building of the responsive context necessary for authentic communication and collaboration.

The importance of both *Sense-Making* and *Appreciating* cannot be overstated. Not only do these strategies cement the respect engendered through *Welcoming* and *Allowing*, they also set the foundation for the final two strategies—*Joining* and *Harmonizing*—which promote the emergence of outcomes that are truly inclusive of diverse perspectives, beliefs, and/or behaviors.

Discussion Questions/Activities

1. The opening paragraph to this chapter contains the following statements: "These strategies are designed to establish reciprocity. They simultaneously build on and facilitate *Welcoming* and *Allowing*." What is your understanding of these statements? How do you think these strategies establish reciprocity? How do they build on and also facilitate *Welcoming* and *Allowing*?

2. Think about a behavior that you cannot understand (e.g., not getting medical care, overspending). Why do you think a person would behave that way? Can you imagine yourself ever behaving the same way? Why or why not?

3. Discuss the following paragraph related to *Sense-Making*: Vigorous disagreeing or even fighting might, for example, make sense to someone if the alternative is perceived to be leaving oneself open to violation—and experience in one's context has proved that perception. In this instance behaviors such as verbal abuse might be associated with protecting boundaries

and thus "make sense" in the same way as our own protective behaviors, though we might not exhibit them ourselves or not exhibit them to the degree as the person using them "against" us. The second part of that sentence is as critical to *Sense-Making* as the first. If we cannot imagine ourselves exhibiting some aspect of another's behavior, it is challenging if not impossible to truly make sense of it. It remains non-sensible, foreign or unimaginable.

4. What do you think is meant by the phrase "blindness of certainty?" Can you think of any examples from your own experience?

5. How can you assess and reflect on the degree to which you are appreciating another's diverse beliefs, behaviors or perspectives?

Chapter 7

Being Responsive: Joining and Harmonizing

"The working hypothesis that seemingly unrelated events may, on some level, be quite intimately related or <u>associated</u> is one of the more powerful tools available to people."
(Childs, 1998)

This chapter completes our general discussion of Skilled Dialogue strategies. It focuses on two final strategies: *Joining* and *Harmonizing*. These strategies embody the responsiveness necessary for making communication and collaboration more than we may, perhaps, envision when differing perspectives are involved. They can quite literally lead to outcomes beyond the limitations of familiar expectations and mindsets (i.e., "miracles").

The contrast between being responsive and being reactive is generally well understood. Less well understood is the contrast between being responsive and simply responding. The latter too often communicates only that I have heard you and am taking what you said into account solely in reference to how it fits or doesn't fit with what I know or what I wish to get done.

As discussed in Chapter 4, being responsive involves communicating in such a way that one person clearly hears another's understanding of and empathy for what he or she just said or did. There is an identifiable difference between communication based solely on how I see a given situation (i.e., responding) and communication based on seeking to see the world as you do (i.e., being responsive). Paradoxically, if we start with the latter, the probability of you getting to see the world as I do increases (Gernsbacher, 2006).

A common and often frustrating experience of the contrast between merely responding and being responsive occurs when one calls a company service number with a specific question or request. It almost seems at times as if the company representatives listen for certain identifiers that will allow them to say "Oh, you are calling about issue 125, I will give you answer 125" even when the caller's concern may not really match that answer. While they address the same topic as the caller (e.g., my vacuum isn't working) and say something related to that issue, what they say does not really communicate an understanding of or sensitivity to either the caller's concern or to the caller's degree of concern. The representatives are, in effect, responding only to *their* perception of the situation while remaining unaware of any aspects of the situation that lie outside that perception. There are, unfortunately, many other examples in an increasingly technologically driven world (e.g., responses from GPS devices).

Unlike responding, responsiveness requires the suspension of fixed assumptions and judgments that lead to hearing things in only one way. When one is responsive what "first appeared as fixed or even rigid begins to appear more dynamic because we are sensing the reality as it is being created [rather than how we assume it is], and we sense our part in creating it" (Senge, Scharmer, Jaworski and Flowers, 2004, p.43). Without suspending our assumptions, we remain unable to perceive anything other than what we expect to perceive or what we are already familiar with.

Being responsive is based on the acknowledgment of connections between "my" view and "yours." Senge, Scharmer, Jaworski and Flowers (2004) put this succinctly: "If you feel you've got a problem to solve that is 'out there' [i.e., not connected to me] and you don't necessarily see or want to see any possible relationship between the 'you' who is trying to solve the problem and what the problem actually is, you may wind up not being able to see the problem accurately, in its fullness" (p. 51). Consequently you will, however unintentionally, end up contributing to maintaining the undesired situation rather than allowing it to shift and perhaps dissolve.

Skilled Dialogue's strategies of *Joining* and *Harmonizing* are designed to engender responsiveness. The first, *Joining,* does this by exploiting the power of the other through choosing relationship. *Harmonizing* then exploits the power of paradox through focusing on the whole underlying the parts (Senge, Scharmer, Jaworski and Flowers, 2004). Both of these strategies tend to be more challenging than the previous ones.

Joining

The strategy of *Joining* deepens the relational perspective developed through *Welcoming* and *Sense-making.* Its goal is to explicitly identify a common substratum between one person's perspectives, beliefs, or behaviors and another's without blurring or eliminating the distinctions between them. Regardless of how totally different and even contradictory one perspective may appear from the other, there is in almost all cases[15] a common substratum.

Joining is marked by two abilities: the ability to truthfully say "I can see myself doing or saying the same thing if I were in your shoes" and the ability to express another's perspectives or beliefs in such a way that, in the estimation of that person, they are accurately represented. Through these abilities, *Joining* invites us to shift our attention from an individual's behaviors, beliefs, and perspectives to the "symphony" they can create when joined with another's (Senge, Scharmer, Jaworski & Flowers, 2004). It focuses our attention on the whole rather than only on the isolated parts and acknowledges that, like single notes, individual perspectives cannot be said to be truly meaningful when apart from their relationship with others' perspectives. Using a different metaphor, *Joining* calls for attending to the "whole" in the same way as does an impressionist painting in which the individual dots of paint have no meaning in and of themselves. It is only when they are attended to as a whole, in relation to each other, that a clear picture emerges (Senge, Scharmer, Jaworski & Flowers, 2004).

What one person says or does in an interaction does not exist independently. To a greater or lesser degree what one person says or does when interacting with another is influenced by how they perceive that other and what he or she is saying or doing (or has said or done in the past). Interacting with someone as someone we believe needs to change, for example, will in all likelihood elicit different words and behaviors from us than interacting with someone from whom we believe we can learn. This "joined" aspect of individuals' perepectives can be difficult to recognize or acknowledge as it is often outside our explicit awareness.

Senge, Scharmer, Jaworski and Flowers (2004) are among the few that comment on the importance of connecting the details of our own actions with others' perspectives, as well as the behaviors and beliefs to which these lead. Being able to join with another's perspective communicates our acknowledgement that we are not isolated from the problems we perceive in others' behaviors, perspectives, and beliefs. This acknowledgement is good news: "If 'we' are creating the problems we have now, then we can create something different" (p. 47).

Joining often first occurs internally as we reflect on whether we have ever behaved, believed, or viewed reality in the same way as the person with whom we are interacting. While we may not have ever refrained from getting a medical check-up, for example, have we neglected self-care in other, perhaps less overt ways? Similarly, we may not ever have explicitly refused to listen to someone, but have we ever not taken someone seriously? Perhaps we cannot identify with someone who is not organized in regard to their external environment. Yet, have we ever been highly distracted and unable to concentrate (i.e., scattered and disorganized)? Or, on the other hand, is our high degree of organization a reaction to our potential disorganization (i.e., we fear we might become totally disorganized)? Is disorganization present as a "shadow" reality that sustains our organization?

Joining does not require that we behave, believe, or see things exactly as someone else does. It does require that we seek to find ways of understanding the validity of things from their perspective. Once we do, *Joining* can be expressed through comments such as "You know, I think I'm doing the same thing. I'm asking you to listen yet I'm not sure I'm really listening to you. Could you please repeat that?" or "I think I too am looking at only one part of what happened while asking you to look at things from my viewpoint. Can you tell me more about how you see things?" A comment such as "I've thought about doing that" can also express *Joining*. At times, even detailed reiterations of the other's perspective may be appropriate (e.g., "I understand just how frustrating it can be when it seems I'm not really hearing you. Let me see if I can restate your concern.").

Assessment questions. Key questions for determining whether we are in fact joining with another include questions such as those below:

"What am I doing or saying that promotes or sustains the current 'problem'?"

(And yes, I am always doing or saying something that does!) This need not always be shared with the other person but does need to be identified.

"Am I communicating implicitly or through subtle messages that I see the others' behaviors, perspectives, or beliefs as something I could never connect with?" For example, am I saying things like "I just can't understand that," or "I can't see how that would be helpful in this situation"—or simply not saying anything that directly acknowledges the other's perspective or concern?

"Am I referencing context or am I acting as if perspectives, behaviors, and beliefs always carry the same meaning regardless of context? A more specific question might be: "What larger context or "script" is linking the other's perspectives, beliefs, or behaviors with my own? If we were in a play, what role might I be playing (e.g., the expert, the organizer, the overwhelmed)? This question is important because each role I play is joined with and sustains a complementary role (e.g., the novice, the disorganized one, or the one who's not taking this seriously). Scripts and the roles they set up limit our ability to be responsive.

Put succinctly, *Joining* is about two people "being on the same page," and communicating that, even when their perspectives and behaviors are quite different. It is a subtle yet critical strategy based on the prior ones (welcoming, allowing, sense-making, and appreciating). Without it *Harmonizing*, Skilled Dialogue's culminating strategy, cannot be implemented.

Harmonizing

Harmonizing challenges us to consider responses or resolutions to a given interaction beyond those we might expect or might imagine. It is a strategy that extends and deepens *Joining* through the integration of separate elements into a whole (i.e., 3rd Space). Put more simply, it is about two (or more) perspectives "played" at the same time similarly to two (or more) musical notes played at the same time so as to create a harmonious chord that neither eliminates nor changes any of the original notes.

The intent of *Harmonizing* is to generating an inclusive and paradoxical space (i.e., 3rd Space) within which the individual strengths of diverse perspectives can be leveraged toward a common goal without either eliminating or devaluing either. Reframing diverse and apparently polarized or contradictory perspectives into paradoxes is a key aspect of *Harmonizing*.

Paradoxes take us beyond limited frames of reference that interpret contrasts as contradictions (i.e., if X and Y are different they must be contradictory). They create new frames that interpret contrasts as complementary rather than contradictory through fostering "double" or binocular view that like physical eyesight can take two distinct perspectives and integrate them into one image.

A simple example of how easily familiar "monocular" frames of reference can blind us to other possibilities is given by Perkins (2000): "There's a man with a mask at home. There's a man coming home. What's going on here?" (p. 29).

Take a minute to consider how you are framing this scenario. Are you picturing the man with a mask as a thief? How are you interpreting "home?" Once you identify your frame, can you come up with other frames?

Three possible "frames" are given by Perkins: (1) a baseball game (the man is a catcher and home is not a house), (2) a surprise costume birthday party (the man is a guest and home is a house) and (3) a flooded home (the man is a diver going underwater to retrieve some items).

Some of these frames, especially the last one, may seem nonsensical. The purpose of identifying multiple frames, however, is not to ascertain immutable truth. It is rather to tap into the "power of uncertainty" (Langer, 2005, p. 15) by bringing to our attention unexpected possibilities. In scanning these possibilities, it becomes easier to keep diverse perspectives, beliefs, and behaviors "on the table" simultaneously without polarizing them into contradictions.

It can admittedly be difficult to reframe contrasting perspectives, beliefs, and behaviors in this fashion. Often it requires repeated brainstorming until the right alignment between perspectives, beliefs, and behaviors can be identified. More information and examples are given in Chapter 8.

Assessment questions. The questions that can help us assess the degree to which *Harmonizing* is present may be categorized into two types. The first type focuses on the degree to which we are open to the possibility of reframing perspectives into paradoxes in the first place. The second focuses on how another's diverse perspective might complement rather than contradict our own.

Questions of the first type include questions such as the following:

"To what degree do I believe the other's perspective, behavior, or belief, no matter how different from my own, can be of value to this situation?"

"To what degree am I open to outcomes other than the one I desire, believe is best or believe is the only possible ones?"

"To what degree am I willing to let go my preference for a dichotomous "your way or my way" interpretation of the perspectives before me? "Do I believe there is an "our way" (i.e., that the other's perspective, behavior, or belief can be integrated with my own in this situation?)"

These three questions are relevant because it is important to first reflect on our willingness to entertain the possibility of paradox and 3rd

Space before we actively seek to harmonize diverse perspectives. If this willingness is not present then any efforts to use *Harmonizing* will fall short of truly integrating diverse perspectives, behaviors, and beliefs.

Once we have assessed our willingness, three additional questions need to be addressed. Questions of this second type directly address how another's specific perspective, behavior, or belief could complement our own. They include question such as the following:

"Is there a common underlying base to the other's perspective, belief, or behavior and my own perspective, belief, or behavior (e.g., do we both want the same thing at a deeper level but are seeing different paths to achieving it?)?

"How might this interaction look like if the respective strengths of each perspective, behavior, belief were integrated rather than polarized?" (Note: those strengths should have been identified through previous strategies.)

"What might your perspective/belief/behavior + my perspective/belief/behavior equal?" or put somewhat differently: "What inclusive option(s) (i.e., 3rd Space) might be created if your perspective/belief/behavior was integrated with my perspective/ belief/behavior?"

Harmonizing takes time and does not come readily, especially when first learning to see things through paradoxical lenses. It may often take a second or even third interaction with someone who holds a diverse perspective to arrive at 3rd Space options. It is perfectly OK at such times to say something like "I'm not sure just how we might be able to honor both our viewpoints, but I am sure that if we put our heads together we can figure something out. Let's think about that and arrange to meet again." Part III shows some examples of what *Harmonizing* might look like in concrete situations. It is important to remember that there is never just one "correct" 3rd Space option. Typically once one has been arrived at, others will also arise.

Discussion Questions/Activities

1. Do you believe that two contradictory things can both be true at the same time? Can you think of example where this is the case? (One possibility: half-full and half-empty)

2. How would you explain *Harmonizing* to someone unfamiliar with Skilled Dialogue?

3. Have you ever created a harmonizing 3rd Space inclusive of two contrasting perspectives or seen that done?

4. Read and discuss these examples of *Harmonizing*:

    a. One member of a team cannot attend a meeting and refuses to agree to anything that might be decided at that meeting. The other members of the team want to make a final decision at that meeting in order to meet a deadline. *Harmonizing* option: Use Skype or Face Time to include members who cannot attend.
    This is only one possible "3rd Space." Can you come up with other responses that reflect *Harmonizing*?

    b. Person A is routinely late to important assignments. His supervisor insists that he must come on time or he will be fired because he cannot demonstrate responsibility. Person A insists that it is not possible for him to arrive on time. What might *Harmonizing* look in this case? Can you brainstorm at least two possible responses?

PART III:
PRACTICE

Chapter 8

Getting the Hang of Paradox and 3rd Space

This chapter explores several key practices common to generating both paradox and 3rd Space: associative thinking, reframing, and brainstorming. These practices, while not exhaustive, have been chosen for their usefulness to *Harmonizing*, the Skilled Dialogue strategy that relies on both paradox and 3rd Space to integrate diverse perspectives and transform their apparent contradictions into complementarities.

Getting the hang of paradox and 3rd Space involves learning to think in ways beyond the typical linear, logical ways that tend to be most common in today's culture. Typical linear, logical ways thinking tend to lead to polarization of differences and, thus, decrease the probability of generating 3rd Space. Nonlinear and seemingly illogical ways of thinking (e.g., associative thinking), on the other hand, decrease the tendency to polarize differences and increase the probability of integrating diverse perspectives.

In one of our earlier books, we presented a short anecdote from Yaconelli's *Dangerous Wonder* (1998) that, in its own way, illustrates the power of paradox and the essence of 3rd Space: connecting and interweaving the different "notes" of diverse perspectives, our own and those of others with whom we interact.

In this anecdote Yaconelli tells a story about a sold out concert by pianist I. J. Paderewski. Thinking to encourage him with his piano lessons, a mother brought her nine-year-old son to this concert. Even before the concert started, however, the little boy started to get restless. The mother tried unsuccessfully to get him to sit still. Unfortunately, in an unguarded moment, he made a run toward the great Steinway piano that was on the stage. He climbed up, sat on the piano bench and began to play "Chopsticks." People in the audience were understandably, or perhaps not so understandably, outraged. Voices could be heard yelling at the boy to stop, yelling at the mother to get him off the stage. Paderewski, who was still backstage, heard the commotion. After discovering what was happening, he stepped onstage. To everyone's amazement, Yaconelli says, "Paderewski came up behind [the little boy], went down on his knees and whispered…'Don't stop. Keep on playing. You're doing great.' While the boy continued…the great pianist put his arms around the boy and began playing a concerto based on the tune 'Chopsticks (p. 145).'" In this same way Skilled Dialogue invites each person in an interaction to keep speaking their perspective as it seeks to connect and encompass differences between them.

Chapter 2 contained some examples of paradox and 3rd Space: the human body, which integrates various organs and body parts that remain distinct; the color green, which integrates blue and yellow without changing the nature of either though they can no longer be perceived individually; a choir, which integrates individual voices while requiring they remain distinct. In all these examples the distinct uniqueness of the integrated parts remains; indeed it is necessary to achieve the resulting 3rd Space. It is this aspect of paradox that is critical to Skilled Dialogue.

See if you can think of other examples before reading on.

Was this easy or not for you?

How comfortable are you thinking in this way?

Thinking paradoxically and creating 3rd Space takes skill and practice. Perhaps more importantly, some degree of playfulness and creativity is also required. Seelig (2012) provides some delightful examples of playful and creative 3rd Space:

"What happens when you cross a checkerboard with a midnight snack? You get edible crackers with the motto 'Beat them and eat them.' What if you cross high-heeled shoes with a tricycle? You get shoes with training wheels." (p. 33).

While admittedly nonsensical, these examples demonstrate the possibility of integrating two apparently irreconcilable realities into a third inclusive reality. How much we can play with what we know to uncover its commonalities in what at first seem to be contradictions is a thinking skill that can be developed just like any other skill. Readers are encouraged to turn to the sources referenced at the end of this chapter.

Holding two diverse ideas in your mind at the same time. The first step to learning how to think paradoxically is to acknowledge the distinctive differences of existing realities (e.g., Chopsticks and classical concerto) while insistently and simultaneously acknowledging—or at least imagining—the *possibility* of unitive realities; e.g., boy and pianist playing one concerto. Childs (1998) proposes the following exercise:

"Picture some goal or result you've been focusing on lately. When you have established a clear picture representing that goal or result, set it aside for a moment and concentrate instead on where you stand now relative to that goal [how far or how close, what stands in your way, what do you need that you may not have]. ...Then, when the picture is reasonably clear, ...bring into your mind that previously formed picture of the goal and *hold it simultaneously* in your consciousness. ...to the extent that you're able to hold both images in your mind at the same time, you will likely sense some part of the energy that resides between the two;" (p. 31) i.e., that links them and holds the possibility of integrating them into complementary rather than contradictory realities. This juxtaposition or association of what is and a vision of what can be lies at the heart of Skilled Dialogue.

Childs (1998) contrasts such associative thinking, which seldom proceeds in a straight or predictable line, with the linear thinking more commonly used in problem-solving. "The working hypothesis that seemingly unrelated [realities] may, on some level, be intimately related or *associated* is one of the more powerful tools..." (p. 52, Childs, 1998). It is a tool essential to Skilled Dialogue, especially in relation to *Harmonizing*.

Associative thinking. One simple way to practice associative thinking toward this end is to connect and combine ideas. Select two different objects, actions or ideas and ask "How are these alike?" For example, how are efficiency and laziness alike? Answer: They are both

83

concerned with using the least amount of energy possible to achieve a particular goal. Can you think of other ways they may be alike?

Here are some variations to try:

1. Look around where you are right now. Find two things, any two things, and ask yourself "How are these alike? See how many different ways you can find in which they are alike.

2. Pick any two pair of words from the list below and ask yourself "How are these alike?"

   Bird   Tractor
   Foot   Car
   Happiness   Grief
   Chaos   Order

   Try the same activity with other words, especially those you think could not possibly be alike in any way.

3. Think of two contrasting ideas (e.g., people should save money; people should take advantage of opportunities even when these are costly). As above, brainstorm ways in which might be complementary rather than contradictory. (Note: focusing on ideas rather than objects is, typically, more difficult)

Reframing. In addition to associative thinking a second practice that is useful to learning paradox and 3rd Space is the practice of reframing. Reframing involves changing the mental lens through which we view a particular thing. This can involve changing the beliefs, values, assumptions or schemas we use to in attributing particular meanings to particular things (e.g., "This behavior means X," "Someone who believes X must be Y kind of person"). The website www.changingminds.org gives the following examples of reframing:

   -- a problem can be reframed as an opportunity
   -- a weakness can be reframed as a strength
   -- an impossibility can be reframed as a near possibility
   -- "against me" can be reframed as "doesn't care"

More concretely, Fletcher and Olwyler, (1992), offer a great practice for learning reframing: the practice of working with personal paradoxes. Here is a brief description of that practice; readers are encouraged to read Fletcher and Olwyler for additional examples and guidelines. (Note: all words or phrases in quotes are taken directly from Fletcher & Olwyler).

1. First, list personal qualities and characteristics. These can include things like the following:
   -- "actions you like to take and roles you like to play" (e.g., "long range planner, risk taker, conformist, competitor, rule-maker")
   -- "words or phrases that would be used to describe you by people who know you" (e.g., "friendly, truthful, reliable, source of new ideas")
   -- "words or phrases that would be used to describe you by someone who doesn't like you" (e.g., self-doubter, procrastinator, self-serving...deceptive")

   More than one word may be used when necessary (e.g., "hard to pin down," challenger of the status quo"). Do not eliminate any descriptions even if you dislike them or don't believe them. Do mark those you like with an L and those you dislike with a D.

2. Second, combine characteristics into contradictory pairs, one you like and one you don't (e.g., "well-organized slob," "insecure tower of strength"). Remember to just be playful as you do this. It will be unfamiliar and may take a bit of time.

3. Finally, select one pair that "seems to describe a core personal conflict with which you struggle." In all likelihood, you will like one-half of the pair more than the other. One side might feel more like a limitation that you've tried to forget or eliminate.

4. Up to this point, you have created paradoxes. You have not yet tapped into their power to create 3rd Space. To do this, requires what Fletcher and Olwyler call "perception shifting." Starting with pairs other than the core personal paradox you came up with in Step 3, do the following

(a) list the positives of the half of the pair you prefer or like most (e.g., energetic might be fun or enthusiastic)

(b) list the negatives of the half you prefer or like most (e.g., energetic might perhaps be overwhelming at times)

(c) list the positives of the half of the pair you don't like or consider negative (e.g., wimp might, for example, also be gentle or careful)

(d) list the negative of the half of the pair you don't like or consider negative (e.g., wimp can mean being a pushover)

(e) now do the same with both sides of the core personal paradox developed in Step 4. Come up with a "high performance oxymoron," the most positive interpretations of both sides of your core personal paradox and a "nightmare oxymoron," the most negative interpretations of both sides of your personal paradox. Some of the examples provided by Fletcher and Olweyer include the following: "hard-working dreamer," "determined wanderer," "spontaneous planner" (p. 27). The purpose of such integration is two-fold: it allows for the best aspects of each quality to be accessed, and, in so doing, provides a balance for the more negative aspects of each quality.

This 4-step exercise illustrates one way to dissolve the "either-or" mindset that leads to polarizing rather than integrating differences. Once we've learned to step outside of a polarizing mindset in regard to the differences within us, it becomes easier to also step outside it in regard to differences between others and ourselves. Creating 3rd Space then becomes more than just a possibility.

Brainstorming. A third practice helpful to developing paradoxical or 3rd Space thinking is brainstorming. Brainstorming is not about generating correct ideas; it is only about generating ideas. Perkins (2000) identifies brainstorming as a type of conceptual roving or roaming with four rules: "no criticism," "keep moving," "piggyback," and "diversify." The first rules out criticism and censoring of ideas as they come up. The second refers to the need to take ideas lightly and not spend too much time on any one; just keep generating them. The time for pondering them and discriminating between them comes later. The third rule refers to associating ideas. Finally, the last rule is a critical one, somewhat related to reframing: break away from familiar assumptions; use different points of view to generate ideas. A good example is a figure he provides titled "Four elephants eating a grapefruit." It shows a square with a circle in the middle and four bar-like elephant trunks pointing to the circle, one on each side of the square. He asks readers to brainstorm how else it might be titled. Some of the alternatives he offers include "Four exclamation points Competing for the Same Dot," "For Very Dramatic Occasions—the Quadruple Exclamation Point," and "Four Bolts Competing for the Same Nut."

Similarly, he presents a riddle: "...A mantel clock that chimed the hours and quarter hours (one chime each quarter hour)...struck twenty-seven times within the span of an hour and one minute... Nothing was wrong with the clock. ...How could that be?" (p. 119). Find some friends and see if you can brainstorm the answer to this riddle. Here are two clues; you will find the answer at the end of this chapter

1. it is critical to diversify (i.e., break away from familiar assumptions and look at the problem from many points of view).
2. The clock struck one hour twice—can you figure out which one and why?

This chapter can only provide a brief introduction to paradoxical and 3rd Space thinking. The next chapters address the latter further, especially in relation to the Skilled Dialogue strategies of *Joining* and *Harmonizing*. Readers may also find additional information from the following resources, some cited in this book and some not.

Recommended Resources

Learning to think paradoxically and generating 3rd Space both involve stretching familiar patterns of thinking. The references below reflect are great resources for doing this. While some may seem somewhat unorthodox we believe you'll nevertheless find them useful. Have fun stretching! (NOTE: Though many of these books are not recent, they remain both relevant and highly useful.)

Childs, C. (1998). *The spirit's terrain: Creativity, activism and transformation*. Boston, MA: Beacon Press

This book explores creativity in both practical and visionary terms. The following quote gives a hint as to its flavor: "But truly creative organizations [and individuals] begin with little or no interest in technique. They instead begin by … envisioning, usually in colorful detail, the genuinely desired result. …They agree to begin with *absolutely no assumed limitations*: they simply will not in the words of Cornel West, 'allow the present circumstances to dictate [their] conception of the future.' But they begin with an honest and accurate accounting of those present circumstances, good and ill, on both visible and invisible levels" (p. 116).

Dobson, T. & Miller, V. (1993). *Aikido in everyday life*. Berkeley, CA: North Atlantic Books

Addresses ways of viewing our conflicts and interpersonal dissonances using visual shapes to illustrate them. Also provides concrete exercises for choosing how to respond to conflicts and dissonances in ways that promote harmony.

Fletcher, J. & Olwyler, K. (1997). *Paradoxical thinking: How to profit from your contradictions*. San Francisco, CA: Berrett-Koehler.

This book has already been alluded to in this chapter. We highly recommend it as we have found that often the dissonance we experience in relation to diverse perspectives mirrors to a greater or lesser extent the dissonance between our own various characteristics.

Fritz, R. (1989). *The path of least resistance: Learning to become the creative force in your own life.* **NY: Fawcett Columbine.**

This book provides detailed discussion of how to work with opposites and contradictions. There is telling statement that captures the core message: "When we think of [situations, behaviors or people] as problems, we try to solve them. When you are solving a problem, you are taking action to have something go away: the *problem*. When you are creating, you are taking action to have something come into being: the *creation* [i.e., the miracle, the 3rd Space]" (p. 11).

Fritz, R. (1991). Creating: *A guide to the creative process.* **NY: Fawcett Columbine.**

This is a later book by Fritz in which he revisits and extends his discussion from the previous one. Learning and practicing the creative process as Fritz describes can be an invaluable support for strengthening both our inclination toward and our skills for Setting the Stage for Miracles.

Perkins, D. (2000). *The eureka effect: The art and logic of breakthrough thinking.* **NY: W.W. Norton.**

This book is referenced in this chapter. "Breakthrough thinking" (i.e., insights into unimagined options, shifts in perception that reveal new paths to desired goals) is essential to Skilled Dialogue. Skilled Dialogue can never be a prescriptive process, with each step mapped out in detail.

Zander, R.S. & Zander, B. (2000). *The art of possibility: Transforming professional and personal life.* **Boston, MA: Harvard Business School.**

"This a how-to book of an unusual kind. ...Our premise is that many of the circumstances that seem ...[problematic]...may only appear so based on a framework of assumptions we carry with us. Draw a different frame around the same set of circumstances [i.e., re-frame them] and new pathways come into view. Find the right framework and extraordinary accomplishment becomes an everyday experience" (p. 1).

Wind, Y. & Crook, C. (2004). *The power of impossible thinking: Transform the business of your life and the life of your business.* **Philadelphia, PA: Wharton School Publishing**

This book addresses mental models and how to identify and shift them. The authors suggest ways of identifying disconfirming information to challenge the familiar mental models that underlie our current understandings. They also talk about "zooming out and looking at the big picture" (p. 103). This "big picture" is what we are referring to when we talk about harmonizing opposites into inclusive paradoxes.

Katie, B. & Mitchell, S. (2002). *Loving what is: Four questions that can change your life.* **NY: Three Rivers Press.**

The four questions addressed in this book are very helpful in learning to reframe our perceptions and judgments about others. The questions can also be accessed through Katie's website www. thework.org.

Seelig, T. (2012). *InGenius: A creative course on creativity.* **NY: HarperOne.**

This book contains many examples of reframing. Its point is that our questions about a situation or problem set a frame that determines the range of possible answers we may find. Examining our questions can thus open the possibilities of multiple answers. Seelig gives a simple example: "What is the sum of 5 plus 5?" as compared to "What two numbers add up to 10?" The first has only one right answer. The second has many possible answers that could all be correct.

Shapiro, D. (2016). *Negotiating the nonnegotiable: How to resolve your most emotionally charged conflicts.* **NY: Viking.**

Shapiro is founder and director of the Harvard International Negotiation Program. He has had extensive experience working with conflicted situations around the world. This book contains a wealth of information on both understanding and resolving emotionally charged conflicts—and aren't all our conflicts emotionally charged? His view is summarized in the following comment: "Jazz finds harmony in dissonance. The dissonance remains, but is held together by a deeper integrative force." An almost exact paraphrase could apply to Skilled Dialogue. Skilled Dialogue finds harmony in differences. The differences remain, held together in a deeper integrative paradox. (Further information and resources on Shapiro's approach to conflict can be found at www.danshapiroglobal.com.

Nonverbal Representations of 3rd Space

Magic Eye books (www.magiceye.com)

These books illustrate a hidden 3-D picture what seems to be a simple 2-D image. They capture the sense of 3rd Space as a reality that is always present but not readily discerned.

Photomosaic Puzzles (www.buffalogames.com)

These puzzles are referenced in our earlier Skilled Dialogue book. Photomosiac puzzles are composed of multiple small pictures that, when joined in the puzzle, form a larger image. They are a fairly exact visual depiction of 3rd Space: a bigger picture that emerges from the integration of smaller elements without in any way changing those smaller elements.

Trust Bridge exercise. This exercise is contained in *An Unused Intelligence: Physical Thinking for the 21st Century* (Bryner and Markova, 1996). The exercise is a marvelous way of physically experiencing 3rd Space. This is the adaptation as we use it to illustrate 3rd Space (all phrases in quotes taken from pp. 91-91):

1. *Invite two people (Person A and Person B) forward. "Person B forms an arched bridge by kneeling on hands and knees. Person A then bends over, and with elbows and forearms leans on B," relying on B for support.*
2. *Ask B to "Suddenly and without notice" collapse. Typically, Person A also collapses as he or she loses B's support. Tell participant this is Option 1.*
3. *In the next step, ask B to again forms a bridge. Ask A to rest his or her arms on B more lightly this time, just in case B collapses again.*

4. *Ask B to once again collapse "Suddenly and without notice." In this case, Person A typically does not collapse. Tell participants this is Option 2.*

5. *The two options illustrate a contradiction between perspectives: dependence and independence.*

6. *After discussing that contradiction ask participants to think about a third option. After several minutes, illustrate that option if no one has come up with it. Ask Person B to once more form a bridge. "Person A then leans over and contacts B with elbows and forearms, simultaneously maintaining a connection with B" and retaining his or her own center of gravity. I tell A that they must place their weight on B <u>and</u> also remain aware of their own balance and center. This may take a while to accomplish.*

7. *As before, ask B to collapse suddenly and without warning. This time, if A has successfully retained their center of gravity and also rested their forearms on B, he or she will typically drop slightly but will not fall. This is Option 3: interdependence Option 3 integrates dependence and independence physically and gives A the physical experience of 3rd Space.* (Interestingly, when done as a verbal exercise in which individuals are asked to come up with a concept that integrates dependence and independence, the majority cannot come up with "interdependence."

Answer to clock riddle: Ordinarily, the clock would strike 12 chimes at 12 and then one at each quarter hour following (12: 15, 12:30, 12: 45). This would only yield 15 chimes. To make it 27 would require 12 additional chimes, meaning that the clock struck 12 twice. But there was nothing wrong with it so why would it do that? Perkins (2000) provides the following answer: "The clock will chime 12 two times within an hour if the owner sets the clock back one hour just before midnight on the night people adjust their clocks back from daylight savings time to standard time." (p. 121)

Chapter 9

Getting the Hang of Skilled Dialogue Strategies

The strategies are the most visible and concrete element of Skilled Dialogue. Table 9.1 shows their relationship with Skilled Dialogue's two dispositions and three qualities. While this framework is relatively simple, the implementation of the strategies can at times appear complex due to their non-linear and interdependent nature. For example, *Welcoming* is a prequel to *Allowing*. At the same time, *Allowing* both deepens and extends *Welcoming*. No strategy is ever truly separate from the others and none can be fully implemented without the others also being implemented.

This chapter contains further information on each strategy. It gives practice activities for each as well as specific examples and non-examples in relation to particular interactions. Readers may find it helpful to read this chapter in conjunction with earlier chapters or may wish to wait until they have familiarized themselves with the more general information on Skilled Dialogue and its strategies before doing so.

While not directly visible, the dispositions underlying our visible behaviors are always discernable to those who interact with us. Welcoming words can, for example, ring false or true depending on whether we use them to truly express desired relationship or only to achieve a desired outcome. The examples and non-examples given below therefore presume the disposition with which they are associated, and which they are intended to express (see Table 9.1).

Three of the Skilled Dialogue strategies—*Welcoming, Sense-Making* and *Joining*—are focused on building and strengthening relationship. They are most closely associated with the disposition of Choosing Relationship over Control. Three others—*Allowing, Appreciating* and *Harmonizing*— focus more specifically on setting up paradox and generating 3rd Space. They are, thus, most closely associated with the disposition of Setting the Stage for Miracles.

The discussion below first focuses on *Welcoming, Sense-Making*, and *Joining*, the strategies associated with the disposition of Choosing Relationship over Control. In actual use, the strategies are most often addressed relative to the qualities they express (see Chapter 10 for illustrations).

Welcoming

<u>Practice Activities</u>

1. How you would greet a friend that you had not seen in a while? What would you say? How would you act? Now think of how you would greet a colleague or co-worker? What would be similar? What would be different?
2. Think of times when you have felt welcomed by someone? What words or actions communicated that welcome? Think of times when you did not feel welcomed by someone. What was different in that situation as compared to the first?
3. Make a list of words and behaviors that you believe are welcoming and a parallel list of words and behaviors you believe are not welcoming. Give the lists to at least two people you know and ask them if they agree. Would they exclude any words or behaviors from one list or the other? Would they add any words or behaviors? Ask them why or why not.

Examples and Non-Examples of Welcoming

Examples	Non-Examples
1. Hello. I'm so glad that you were able to come. How has your week been?	1. "Thanks for coming. Have you thought about what I mentioned on the phone?"
2. Thanks for coming. I'm really looking your thoughts about our project.	2. "I'm glad you're here. As you know, it's been a rough week and we need to get started on our project as soon as possible.
3. So good to see you. I hope you didn't have any problem finding this room. I am really looking forward to hearing your ideas on how we can improve. Your expereince is such as asset for us.	3. Hello. Sorry I'm late. I had such a hard time getting here. The traffic was really heavy and then I couldn't find a parking place. ...

Sense-Making

Practice Activities

1. Review the pairs of behaviors below. Brainstorm at least 3 ways in which the behavior you believe most negative makes sense and can be of value.

   long range planning ----- spur of the moment action

   conformist behavior ---- individualist behavior

   organization ---- disorganization

   socially oriented behavior --- non-social or loner behavior

   Choose other behavior pairs and brainstorm how those you find negative or irritating an make sense and be of value.

2. Get into groups of two and reflect on the following statements: Taking drugs can be helpful when one is feeling ill. Can you think of at least 3 other situations in which it would make sense to take drugs?

   Arriving late to an appointment can be helpful in making time for unexpected tasks. Can you think of at least 3 other situations in which arriving late would make sense?

Think of other behaviors that you believe are inappropriate or don't make sense. Brainstorm what circumstances within which they would make sense and be of value.

3. Observe situations in your work and social settings. Can you find examples of *Sense-Making* or lack thereof? Describe one interaction where this strategy was clearly present and one where it was not. What was different?

Examples and Non-Examples

Examples	Non-Examples
1. Can you tell me more about why you think that would be a good way to do this?	1. That doesn't make any sense to me. I'm not sure it would work.
2. I've never thought of it that way. Can you tell me more?	2. I think it might be better if…
3. "That is an interesting suggestion, tell me about how that would work." "What would be your next steps?"	3. "Why don't you just tell him he is wrong?"
4. "That is really a thought-provoking idea!" "How do you see it taking place?"	4. "I have a better idea, why don't you just ….."

Joining

Practice Activities

1. Select a behavior or viewpoint with which you disagree. These often involve money, time or organization (e.g., chronic lateness or compulsive timeliness; saving or not saving money; cluttered or non-cluttered work areas). If you (Person B) were meeting with someone (Person A) who behaved that way or held the belief that it was OK to behave that way (e.g., not save money), could you argue for that behavior or viewpoint, whether or not you agreed with it? Role-play doing that then ask person A to rate how well they believe you represented their view or

behavior. (Another way to do this activity is to role-play one side with someone roleplaying the other and then switch sides and repeat the role play.)

2. Watch a television movie or sitcom. Select an extended interaction or conversation between individuals holding different views, beliefs, opinions or values. To what degree was one individual in that interaction or conversation able to join with the other (i.e., represent their views, beliefs, opinions or values)?

   (lo)   2   **3** (some)   4   **5** (high)

   Describe behaviors/actions in support of your rating.

Examples and Non-Examples

Examples	Non-Examples
1. "Perfect, I think that we are on the same page."	1. "Here is what I think is happening."
2. "It's clear to me that we are both very concerned about this situation."	2. "I'm surprised that you aren't aware of the problem; it seems very evident to all of us."
3. "I can hear your frustration with this situation. I know how unpleasant it can be."	3. "I'm concerned about Peter. I have talked with several other people. They seem to think he is having a problem too."

Let's switch now to strategies in this section associated with Setting the Stage for Miracles: *Allowing, Appreciating,* and *Harmonizing.* These are, in some ways, more challenging than the previous ones because they invite us to enlarge our frames of reference.

Allowing

Practice Activities

1. Form groups of three. One person will be an observer and note-taker, the other two will role play a 10 minute conversation

where one comes to discuss a problem with the other (e.g., the need to take time off, disagreement with a co-worker). Rate the degree to which you believe you each allow the other to express him/herself without interrupting or defending your own views.

(lo)　　2　　**3** (some)　　4　　**5** (high)

List specific behaviors/actions that supported your rating. Debrief with observer note-taker. Does he or she agree with your ratings? Why or why not? Repeat the roleplay and see if you can increase your ratings.

Examples and Non-Examples

Examples	Non-Examples
1. I see. Can you tell me more about that? 2. I understand. 3. Listen w/o verbal comments and with nonverbal signs of attention and interest	1. I see. What would you think about doing it this way? 2. I think we need to look at things differently. 3. What do you think about the suggestions I emailed you?

Appreciating

Practice Activities

Form groups of three. One person will be an observer and note-taker, the other two will role play a 10 minute conversation where one comes to discuss a concern with the other (e.g., the need to take time off, disagreement with a co-worker). After the conversation, debrief with observer/note-taker and rate the conversation:

(lo)　　2　　**3** (some)　　4　　**5** (high)

To what degree were you each able to appreciate the other's views? List specific behaviors/actions that supported or limited *Appreciating*. What would you do differently if you were to repeat the role-play?

Examples and Non-Examples

Examples	Non-Examples
1. I see. I understand how doing/thinking that can be of value in your situation.	1. I hear what you're saying. I just don't think it can help in this situation.
2. You know, I think I'd do something much like that if I were in your shoes.	2. "I'd never do that." (thought, not spoken aloud).
3. I can see how doing/thinking that has helped in the past.	3. Have you thought of doing something that might be more productive?

Harmonizing

Practice Activities

1. Form groups of three. One person will be an observer and note-taker, the other two will role play a 10 minute conversation where one comes to discuss a problem with the other (e.g., the need to take time off, disagreement with a co-worker). Decide on specific roles (e.g., supervisor, friend, co-worker). After the conversation, debrief with observer note-taker and rate the conversation:

    (lo)   2   **3** (some)   4   **5** (high)

To what degree were you each able to integrate the other's views so as to generate complementary and inclusive response options? List specific behaviors/actions that supported or limited *Harmonizing*.

Examples and Non-Examples

Examples	Non-Examples
1. "What if we could do both things?" "What do you think that might look like?" 2. "I think we can let Peter participate in the activities with his peers as you are suggesting and also provide some of the more specialized 1:1 time with his therapist. One could actually help the other."	1. As we just discussed, we believe that Peter really needs 1:1 time with his therapist instead of time in group activities with his peers." 2. "I understand that you'd like something different than what we are proposing, but I don't see how that can be possible at this time."

Table 9.1 Skilled Dialogue Strategies with Associated Behaviors

	Choosing Relationship over Control	Setting the Stage for Miracles
RESPECT Key Dynamic: Affirmation of other's boundaries	WELCOMING *Express interest in meeting with other (e.g., I'm glad we have this opportunity; I'm looking forward to hearing your views on this matter);*	ALLOWING *Listen, listen, listen w/o interrupting or interjecting alternative perspective share verbal indicators of nonjudgmental attention (e.g., "I see", "That's interesting");*
RECIPROCITY **Key Dynamic: Power equalizing**	**SENSE-MAKING** *Prompt other(s) to tbout their perspective; (e.g., Can you tell me more about that?" "What do you think would happen if you didn't do/see/believe that?" "Let me see if I understand, are you saying...?"); equalize" participation: use language familiar to other, or unfamiliar to both so that at same cognitive level*	**APPRECIATING** *Explicitly acknowledge validity of other's perspective (e.g., "That must have been really difficult"); name the strengths of diverse perspective ("I can see how that might be an effective strategy under the circumstances); communicate "you're right" and I'm right" paradox*

	JOINING	*HARMONIZING*
RESPONSIVENESS Key Dynamic: Linking and integrating differences	*Explicitly dentify connections between your perspective and other's perspective (e.g., "I've thought about doing that;" "I do something similar;" "Let me see if I understand... is this what you're saying?")*	Prompt for inclusive options (e.g., "If we thought of it as your having one half of the whole picture and I held the other half, what might the whole picture look like?" "You have an important and necessary part of the picture; I believe I do also; how can we put the two together to form a whole?"); Explore how contradictory perspectives can be complementary; (e.g., 2 notes = chord); reframe (i.e., restate situation from different perspectives; offer multiple interpretations)

Chapter 10

Putting It All Together

This chapter contains four distinct sections. The first frames Skilled Dialogue generally, using the yin/yang symbol. The second illustrates what Skilled Dialogue can look like more specifically through the discussion of a "master example" that contains all its elements. The third section revisits each strategy as it lists the procedural steps involved in using Skilled Dialogue. Finally, the fourth section contains several practice scenarios.

THE YIN-YANG OF SKILLED DIALOGUE [16]

Skilled Dialogue starts with the identification of two contrasting points of view that appear to be contradictory or irreconcilable and allow only an either-or choice. If one point of view is favored or chosen, the other must be excluded or minimized, leaving the people involved with access to only half of what is possible. At this point, attention to the dispositions is critical. It becomes important to ask whether the persons involved are disposed toward relationship or control, toward pre-determined outcomes or toward unexpected ones. If they are disposed toward relationship, Skilled Dialogue begins.

It continues as the effort to align or reconcile these contrasting points of view is initiated through the strategies of *Welcoming* and *Allowing*. These both welcome and allow the contrasting points of view with no need to minimize or eliminate one over the other. The two points of view are no longer seen as at odds with each other.

Once welcomed and allowed, the third phase of Skilled Dialogue involves seeking ways to make sense of and appreciate each point of view vis-à-vis the other. This phase is necessary in order to determine and access the strengths of each point of view. "What can each contribute?" becomes the key question. It is at this point that aspects of one point of view can be perceived in the other.

The fourth and final phase involves the intentional crafting of an inclusive "3ʳᵈ Space," which encompasses both points of view. It is at this that point the strategies of *Joining* and *Harmonizing* come into play in order to bring out and integrate the complementary strengths of each point of view. This fourth figure represents the key aspects of Skilled Dialogue:

1. Each point of view remains distinct (e.g. black remains black and white remains white).
2. Both are connected along their borders
3. Each contains a "seed" of the other
4. And, finally, an inclusive whole, signified by border in bold, is created through their integration.

EXAMPLE OF SKILLED DIALOGUE

The sample case used in this section is adapted from a scenario described by Cynthia Bourgeault as she discusses holding the tension of opposites through the Law of Three (Bourgeault, 2013). While the Law of Three is not equivalent to 3rd Space as the term is used in Skilled Dialogue, the scenario she describes in her discussion provides an excellent template for looking at Skilled Dialogue and its strategies more closely.

It is a scenario that has all the markings of a classic "my way or your way" interaction. It involves a director of a small service agency who needs to go before the requisite Board to justify her budget and request funds for the following year. The Board is, of course, charged with approving or disapproving both how funds have been spent and how Directors propose to spend them in the coming year. Like most years, board members are looking to cut expenditures in order to have enough to meet rising costs of necessary expenses such as space and utilities. The director has witnessed several other directors who had come before her have "over-expenditures" pointed out to them and be turned down for any requested increases. A power struggle seems inevitable as her turn comes. Then, as put by Bourgeault, "inspiration arrived." It is in the director's behavior consequent to that inspiration that Skilled Dialogue best be illustrated.

First, the director thanks the Board for the funds they allotted to her agency the previous year. In doing this she communicates respect for their decision-making. She clearly *welcomes* the opportunity to interact with them once more while simultaneously *allowing* them to act as they deem appropriate. Additionally, she indirectly communicates that their decisions *make sense* and that she can *appreciate* them, thus setting up a reciprocal context.

Second, she continues by saying that she is not asking for any additional funds and, in fact, has a strategy in place should they need to cut back. In doing this, the director effectively *joins* with the Board, representing their position from their perspective. She clearly is responsive to their concerns and implies that she recognizes their responsiveness to hers as well.

Skilled Dialogue's final strategy, *harmonizing*, is left largely undefined in this scenario though it can be implied. In stating that she has no-new-funds strategy ready to go, the director communicates clearly that her needs as well as the Board's can be met even if no additional funds are forthcoming. By illustrating her use of current funds, she also alludes that this can also be done if additional funds are forthcoming. In the end, she communicates that her needs and the Board's needs can be in harmony one way or the other.

This scenario has been chosen as an example of Skilled Dialogue because it both illustrates its strategies and points out the importance of its dispositions of Choosing Relationship over Control and Setting the Stage for Miracles. It is clear from the director's approach that she is focused on choosing relationship with the Board rather than trying to control their response. She is also putting into place what she believes is necessary to set the stage for what might not seem predictable from existing circumstances. As long as Skilled Dialogue dispositions are in place, as they are in the scenario, the individual strategies need not be as explicit or direct as our descriptions of them have been.

> Discuss this scenario. To what degree do you agree that it reflects Skilled Dialogue? Why or why not?

PROCEDURAL STEPS

Skilled Dialogue is a circular and reiterative process not a linear one. Though *Welcoming* and *Allowing* are almost always first, the other four strategies need not be followed in strict sequence. When, for example, it seems difficult to *Appreciate*, it may be necessary to go back to gather more information (i.e., *Sense-Making*) or listen more carefully (i.e., *Allowing*). Similarly, at times it may be necessary to reinforce our disposition to Set the Stage through its strategies before we can authentically Choose Relationship and use its strategies (e.g., if we believe that another's views contradict our own, it will be more difficult to make sense of them or to join with them.

Remember also that, as previously stated, Skilled Dialogue is not the best or most appropriate approach to all interactions. The following 4-step "horizontal" sequence is one that has proven effective in first learning Skilled Dialogue:

Step 1: Setting the dispositions.

Approach the interaction as a relational one rather than one in which you seek to influence or control another or get them to agree with you or help you out.

CHOOSING RELATIONSHIP OVER CONTROL	SETTING THE STAGE FOR MIRACLES
Am I disposed to prioritize my relationship with this person(s) more than my preset agenda (i.e., choose relationship over control)? (lo)　2　**3** (some)　4　**5** (high)	Am I open to outcomes other than those I am anticipating based on what I know now (i.e., disposed to Set the Stage for Miracles)? (lo)　2　**3** (some)　4　**5** (high)

Step 2: Honoring Identity

Welcoming: Communicate verbally and nonverbally that you welcome the interaction as an opportunity to get to know the other and learn from him or her.

Allowing: Allow the other to express their concern or viewpoint without interruption other than to ask for clarification if this is needed. Do not interject your own concerns or views. Simply listen with interest.

Welcoming	**Allowing**
To what degree do I believe I welcomed the other as someone I could learn from? (lo)　2　**3** (some)　4　**5** (high)	To what degree did I allow the other to express him/herself without interrupting or explaining/defending my own views? (lo)　2　**3** (some)　4　**5** (high)

Step 3: Establishing Reciprocity

Sense-Making: Seek to understand how the other's perspective or behavior makes sense. Do this until you can honestly say you understand how such a perspective or behavior makes sense (i.e., is valid) under certain circumstances and that you might do the same or similar under those circumstances.

Appreciating: Identify positive contributions that the other's perspective or behavior might bring to your interaction with them.

Sense-Making	Appreciating
To what degree was I able to make sense of the other's views as valid and evidence-based? (lo) 2 **3** (some) 4 **5** (high)	To what degree was I able to appreciate the other's views as something that could make a positive contribution to our interaction? (lo) 2 **3** (some) 4 **5** (high)

Step 4: Being Responsive

Joining: Find common ground by communicating your understanding of the other's perspective.

Harmonizing: Craft a "third choice" that includes both your and the other's perspectives.

Joining	Harmonizing
To what degree was I able to express the other's views in ways that the other felt were accurate and valid? (lo) 2 **3** (some) 4 **5** (high)	To what degree was I able to integrate the other's views with my own so as to generate response options that were complementary and inclusive of both? (lo) 2 **3** (some) 4 **5** (high)

SHAPES Activity—A Simulation of Skilled Dialogue's Procedural Steps

(Adapted from an activity done by Tim Burns; date and exact source unknown)

This activity is a great way to practice all of the steps just described. It was developed for use in Skilled Dialogue workshops and is modified for use in this book. It can be done in pairs but is best done in groups of 3 or 4. For the purpose of this activity, four different shapes— circle, triangle, square, squiggly (a squiggly line)—are used to represent typical differences between people's approach to work. In all cases, as many shapes as possible should be represented within each group. The following characteristics are associated with each shape:

Circle: ties up loose ends, likes closed systems, highly social, well-rounded, nonlinear, talkative, outgoing, networker, likes to include everyone

Square: thinks inside the box, rigid/structured/linear thinking, black & white thinker, authoritative, predictable, low risk-taker, worker bee, salt of the earth

Triangle: balanced, analytical, driven, always in motion, gets things done—in own way, can tell them what to do but don't tell them how

Squiggly: unpredictable, fluid, feel they don't fit, flexible, inventive/creative, think outside the box, always take the scenic route, don't travel in straight lines

Instructions:

1: Ask participants to identify the shape they think best describes them. Clues: "Circles" will often have the hardest time identifying their shape because they don't like to stand out or be different! "Squigglies" have often learned a second shape in order to fit into their chosen professions if these require them to do so. "Squares" are often the worker bees. "Triangles" are also productive but prefer to work on their own.

2: Form small groups (size depends on size of total group; small groups of 3-6 are recommended). At least 3 of the 4 shapes must be represented in each group. Note: it is usually good not to include more than one "circle" in a group as circles tend to dislike differentiation and will often insist there are no real differences.

3: Ask group members to select an issue to explore on which they are likely to differ (e.g., being on time, spending) and briefly discuss their point of view. Explore underlying motivations when there seems to be little difference between individuals holding different shapes. If, for example, individuals say "we all like to be on time" consider why (e.g., "I like to be on time so as not to inconvenience others"—usually a circle response; "I like to be on time because I don't like to waste time"—usually a triangle response; "I like to be on time because it's important to be on time"—usually a square response. Note: Squiggles usually are not very time-oriented at all and can be late because they forget time completely!

4: Stop and debrief experience after 10-15 minutes individually or in the groups in which you did the role play. Use the following worksheet as a guide. Discuss Skilled Dialogue strategies in relation to the interactions between participants. Was there evidence of one more than the others? Was any one totally absent? Did some shapes tend to use one or two strategies more than others? Did any not use some strategies at all?

5: Form into large group once again. Discuss analyses. What did everyone agree on? What were points of disagreement? What might you change if repeating the role play?

Welcoming To what degree do I believe that I welcomed the other? (lo) 2 **3** (some) 4 **5** (high) Behaviors/actions that supported or limited this strategy:	**Allow**ing To what degree did I allow the other to express him/herself without interrupting or defending my own views?) (low) 2 **3** (some) 4 **5** (high) Behaviors/actions that supported or limited this strategy:
Sense-Making To what degree was I able to make sense of the other's views as valid and evidence-based? (low) 2 **3** (some) 4 **5** (high) Behaviors/actions that supported or limited this strategy:	**Appreciating** To what degree was I able to appreciate the other's views? (low) 2 **3** (some) 4 **5** (high) Behaviors/actions that supported or limited this strategy:
Joining To what degree was I able to express the other's views in ways that the other felt were valid? (low) 2 **3** (some) 4 **5** (high) Behaviors/actions that supported or limited this strategy:	**Harmonizing** To what degree was I able to integrate other's and my own views so as to generate response options complementary and inclusive of both? (low) 2 **3** (some) 4 **5** (high) Behaviors/actions that supported or limited this strategy:

PRACTICE SCENARIOS

SCENARIO # I

The Skilled Dialogue strategies have been identified for you in this first scenario. Read the information and then brainstorm your thoughts with a partner or group. (Use Table 10.1 for reference).

Background Information

Dr. Romano, a school principal, introduced a new approach to professional development to his teachers. He asked them to create teams of four teachers to meet and decide on one area of instructional improvement or research focus for the coming year. David was chosen as facilitator by his team, which included Kate, Susan and Daniel, all experienced teachers who had worked closely together for several years. Over the next three months, Dr. Romano tells them, they are to collaboratively develop a unit of lesson plans based on peer observations. The same lesson is to be taught by each teacher while being observed by the other three teachers. After that they are meet to share their observations, provide feedback, and develop an action plan targeting lesson improvement.

Daniel strongly disagrees to being observed by his peers. He states that he prefers observation by the site administrator. Though he participated in the development of the original lesson plans, he doesn't wish to participate in the scheduling of his peer observation. The group's development and submission of their final action plan is consequently being delayed. David, the group facilitator, knows Daniel is a popular and effective teacher with students and parents, so he can't understand why Daniel is having this response to observations by his peers.

Isaura Barrera, Ph.D. & Lucinda Kramer, Ph.D.

INTERACTION	ANALYSIS
David feels frustrated by Daniel's unwillingness to be observed by his peers and wants to get Daniel to change his mind so that his observations can be scheduled and the group can move on. He decides to meet with him one on one.	<u>Choosing Relationship over Control</u>: It is obvious that David's initiation of his first interaction with Daniel is more focused on control (e.g., I want him to change his mind) rather then relationship (e.g., how can I get to know him so that we can work together). He is ready to "tell" Daniel what he needs to do. It is only towards the end of their interaction that he begins to refocus his intention on relationship rather than control. <u>Setting the Stage for Miracles</u>: In the beginning, David is only seeking to change Daniel's mind about being observed by peers. The emergence of this disposition might, though be implied toward the end of David's meeting with Daniel as they begin to work more collaboratively. **Strategies** (NOTE: Numbers in this column correlate with numbers on the left hand column)
"We have to talk," David said when the last student had left Daniel's classroom. "I need a date for your peer observation of the first lesson plan. We need to get moving on this project." (1)	(1) **WELCOMING**: *Not present at all. David believed that he already understood Daniel and he was just not being supportive of the group and was stubborn.*

I know you are not crazy about peer observations, but it's what we need to do." (2)

(2) ALLOWING: Not present at this time.

"Why you are so against this peer teaching observation?" (3)

(3) SENSE-MAKING: While this sounds like the initiation of Sense-Making by David, his tone makes it clear that he is already convinced that Daniel's views made no sense and had no value.

"David, I just didn't expect the observation would be so formal, that you all would be taking notes and completing an observation form on my teaching. I don't like peer reviews, people either like you or they don't, that is how it works. It's not about teaching at all. I went through this in student teaching years ago, it all about if the person likes you, not your teaching." David continued speaking for some time about his beliefs about his teaching observations, what worked and what didn't and gave examples of how peer feedback never improved his teaching.(4)

(4) SENSE-MAKING: David discusses his perspective again with the hope it would make sense to Daniel.
Daniel starts to discuss his perspective in greater depth, opening the door for David to make sense of his response.

Daniel listened without interrupting (5)

(5) ALLOWING: Daniel allows David to state his perspective and experience without interruption. In the sense Allowing is present. (NOTE: If however, he was only doing this to shoot it down, it would not be truly Allowing.)

Daniel tells Daniel that the only positive experience and meaningful feedback on his teaching has come from administrators, never peers. He shares his experiences and beliefs about "peer input" during his teacher preparation program. David listened without interrupting. (6)

(6) ALLOWING: David listened to Daniel without judgment or interruption.

As he listens, David suddenly remembered a teaching observation his first year of teaching, completed by a fellow grade level teacher. He remembered exactly how rejected he felt when her "report" was returned with "needs improvement" checked on each element of teaching and classroom management. He avoided working with her in the future. He remembers it took him a long time to trust and share his teaching with colleagues after that experience. May be he was being to demanding with Daniel. (7)

(7) APPRECIATING: David's listening led him to remember his own unpleasant experience and thus he began to appreciate Daniel's perspective (i.e., to appreciate where he might be coming from). It also led him to appreciate the impact of his own behavior towards Daniel.

"I can see why you don't want to have all of us observe your teaching," David responds. "I know; I have had peer observations that I thought were unfair, they stressed me too. They didn't reflect my teaching and what the students' learned." (8)

(8) JOINING: David acknowledged Daniel's concern and "joined" him in understanding how stressful peer observations can be. (NOTE: Joining extends Sense-Making and Appreciating by moving participate into common ground.)

Daniel replied, "I know, I want to improve my teaching, but not this way. It just not worthwhile feedback." (9)

"Daniel, I can see you are a dedicated teacher and always looking for new ways to teach and support your students. It sounds like we need to find a way to make the observations more useful and try to remove any personal biases of the other teachers as much as possible. That way you might gain some new insights to your teaching strategies in a respectful collegial environment as well as complete this project. What do you think? Can you think of a way we could change the observation process or the observation form? What do you like about administrative observations? Maybe we can use some of those ideas. (10)

(They continue talking for some time, both now confident of finding a way that both the group's and Daniel's needs can be met)

(9) This comments affirms that Joining has occurred.

(10) **HARMONIZING***: David began to introduce the idea of Harmonizing Daniel's desire of a "fair" teaching observation with the group's goal of completing the professional development project. He communicated that one did not necessarily be at odds with the other and prompted for concrete suggestions.*

SCENARIO # 2

The Skilled Dialogue strategies are not identified in this scenario. Can you identify them? Use Scenario #1 as a template for how to complete the table using the given information.

Background Information

Grade level teachers observe a lesson plan in other same grade classrooms, looking carefully at student work and classroom artifacts, talking with students and completing a rubric. The administrator's goal is for them to learn from each other and provide support for novice teachers. However, novice teachers complain that they are being treated like 'student teachers.' They say that they do not find experienced teachers' recommendations to be relevant to their teaching goals. Examples: too much emphasis on state standards (content knowledge) and not the social-emotional development of the student. Special education teachers are especially uncomfortable with the approach, as they believe the other grade level teachers don't understand the differing instructional and behavioral strategies they are required to implement. Rosemary, one of the special education teachers, asks to meet with the campus administrator to discuss her concerns.

INTERACTION	ANALYSIS
NOTE: The segments of description are not aligned with strategies in right hand column. You will need to align them as you think appropriate.	**NOTE**: This case is not designed as a "perfect" case. Please comment on what you see is present as well as what you think should be present but is not.

Setting Dispositions

(<u>Directions</u>: Following the format shown in Scenario #1, briefly discuss statement(s) that you believe represents the named disposition below.

<u>Description of Interaction</u>

Rosemary and Mrs. Brown, the campus administrator, meet in Mrs. Brown's office to discuss Sarah's concerns about the mentoring format being used.

<u>Choosing Relationship over Control</u>:

"Good morning, Rosemary. Please sit." (She points to chair in front of her desk). I'm happy you've given me this opportunity to explain the mentoring model I've chosen for our campus.

<u>Setting the Stage for Miracles</u>:

"I'm glad to be meeting with you, Mrs. Brown. As you know I have some concerns about how you are asking senior staff to work with us."

"I understand Rosemary. Let me tell you a bit about my side of things and then you can share your concerns with me."

"I think it would help if I expressed my concerns first. That way you could address them as you talk about your model."

"OK. First let me tell you why I chose this model." (Mrs. Brown then goes on to describe the evidence base for the model. Rosemary looks uncomfortable but remains silent.)

Thank you for that explanation, Mrs. Brown. There seems to be little evidence for its application in special education settings, however. I have two specific concerns. First, their emphasis on state standards doesn't seem to take special education standards into account. When I've tried to point that out to the teacher who observed me she seemed to treat me as a student teacher with little experience."

Strategies

(Directions: Following the format shown in Scenario #1, number and briefly discuss statement(s) that you believe represent(s) the named strategy. If no statements that support a strategy can be found, state that. Explain why interaction does not reflect these and provide an example of how that strategy might have been used.)

WELCOMING

ALLOWING

SENSE-MAKING

APPRECIATING

JOINING

HARMONIZING

"I'm sorry, Rosemary. I'm sure she didn't mean to come across like that. It's just that they are so concerned about doing their job well and the state standards are so important to us as a school looking to improve."

"Mrs. Brown, do you think there is any need to address special education standards when observing lessons that involve special education students?"

"I believe that all students must meet state standards, of course. I'm not sure how those would be different for the lessons you conduct."

"I see. Perhaps we can meet again after you've had more time to think more about my concerns. I realize this may have been a bit sudden. Thank you." (Rosemary stands up to leave)

"Certainly, Rosemary. I enjoyed our discussion today. I hope it's helped."

SCENARIOS # 3-4

These scenarios provide only general information on certain interactions. On your own, with a partner or in a group, see if you can develop a possible script to describe what might have happened in each one. Place it in a two-column table with the script in the left-hand column and the Skilled Dialogue strategies you used in the right-hand column as in Scenario 1. Discuss why and how you think the strategies were present as was done in Scenario 1.

Scenario # 3:

Sarah is the new executive director of a long established private preschool with three campuses. She was hired to "turn around the school." Her leadership commitment to the board is to present a clear signal that significant change is urgently needed, (2) maintain a consistent focus on improving instruction, (3) make visible improvements quickly, and (4) build teacher group that is committed to the school's improvement goals. She spent the summer visiting each campus and meeting most of the teachers and staff to introduce the new direction the school was taking. At the beginning of the school year, she rolled out her plan at the August Back to School Teacher and Staff Assembly. The reception was flat and the following Q & A was awkward with a general tone of "…everything is fine, don't change what we do." In response, Sarah decides to schedule meetings with 2-3 teachers at a time to further explore what might have happened.

INSTRUCTIONS: Imagine you are Sarah. What would you say or do at one of these meetings? Develop a script describing a meeting. Did you apply each of the Skilled Dialogue strategies? Create a table using the tables in Scenarios 1 and 2 as a guide.

Alternately, imagine you are one of the teachers meeting with Sarah. You were not happy with the outcome of your meeting and decide to schedule another one to meet with her individually to express your concerns. Develop a script describing that individual meeting. Did you apply each of the Skilled Dialogue strategies? Create a table using the tables in Scenarios 1 and 2 as a guide.

Scenario # 4:

Several parents asked Kelly, a teacher at a private preschool, how their child was doing. They were concerned at what they saw as a lack of structured instruction and formal testing of the children's print-based reading and writing skills, which were critically important to them. The teacher primarily used informal instructional and assessment approach, as did most teachers at this preschool. It was a challenge for Kelly and the school director to explain how literacy instruction and assessment, while not evident as isolated activities, did occur within multiple activities during the day. The parents wanted more visible evidence of both. How can Kelly and her director use SD to address this competing parent concern?

INSTRUCTIONS: Imagine you are one of the parents in this scenario and have scheduled a meeting with Kelly and/or the school director. Develop a script describing this meeting. How did you apply each of the Skilled Dialogue strategies? Create a table using the tables in Scenarios 1 and 2 as a guide.

Alternately, imagine you are Kelly meeting with one of the parents. It is important to be able to see a situation from multiple perspectives. Develop a script describing this meeting. How did you apply each of the Skilled Dialogue strategies? Create a table using the tables in Scenarios 1 and 2 as a guide.

Other scenarios:

The scenarios above describe common situations you might encounter as a teacher or administrator. Skilled Dialogue, however, is not limited to work scenarios. Recall an interaction you've had with someone who disagreed with you or who wouldn't listen to you, perhaps a friend, a family member or someone at a business. Then do the following:

1. Describe the context (setting, purpose of interaction, what you hoped would happen, how you wanted interaction to go, participants, etc.)
2. Recreate the interaction as it actually happened and complete a table as for the previous scenarios. Can you identify which strategies were present and which were not? How might you redo the interaction to include all the strategies? How do you think that might affect the outcome?
3. Describe what you would do differently, if anything, now that you know the Skilled Dialogue model.

Table 10.1. Skilled Dialogue Strategies with Associated Behaviors

	Choosing Relationship over Control	Setting the Stage for Miracles
RESPECT Key Dynamic: Affirmation of other's boundaries	WELCOMING *Express interest in meeting with other (e.g., I'm glad we have this opportunity; I'm looking forward to hearing your views on this matter)*	ALLOWING *Listen, listen, listen w/o interrupting or interjecting alternative perspective share verbal indicators of nonjudgmental attention (e.g., "I see", "That's interesting")*
RECIPROCITY Key Dynamic: Power equalizing	SENSE-MAKING *Prompt other(s) to talk about their perspective; (e.g., Can you tell me more about that?" "What do you think would happen if you didn't do/see/believe that?" "Let me see if I understand, are you saying...?"); equalize" participation: use language familiar to other, or unfamiliar to both so that both are at same cognitive level*	APPRECIATING *Explicitly acknowledge validity of other's perspective (e.g., "That must have been really difficult"); name the strengths of diverse perspective ("I can see how that might be an effective strategy under the circumstances); communicate "you're right" and I'm right" paradox*

RESPONSIVENESS	*JOINING*	*HARMONIZING*
<u>Key Dynamic</u>: Linking and integrating differences	*Explicitly identify connections between your perspective and other's perspective (e.g., "I've thought about doing that;" "I do something similar;" "Let me see if I understand… is this what you're saying?")*	*Prompt for inclusive options (e.g., "If we thought of it as your having one half of the whole picture and I held the other half, what might the whole picture look like?" "You have an important and necessary part of the picture; I believe I do also; how can we put the two together to form a whole?"); Explore how contradictory perspectives can be complementary; (e.g., 2 notes = chord); reframe (i.e., restate situation from different perspectives; offer multiple interpretations)*

Chapter 11

Skilled Dialogue Forms

This chapter contains forms that the authors have developed to teach Skilled Dialogue. These include the following: a Self-Assessment (Table 11.1), a Skilled Dialogue Guide to Dispositions and Qualities (Table 11.2), and an Interaction Analysis Form (Table 11.3).

Self-Assessment. This form provides a means of assessing one's skill level in relation to the use of Skilled Dialogue. It is not designed to be a formal measure but rather to provide a qualitative description of how well one has learned Skilled Dialogue and what yet remains to be learned.

Skilled Dialogue Guide to Dispositions and Qualities. This Guide provides a general overview of Skilled Dialogue dispositions and qualities. It is designed as a "Tip Sheet" for quick review when practicing Skilled Dialogue.

Interaction Analysis Form. This form is intended to be used as a guide to reflecting on a past interaction and analyzing the degree to which Skilled Dialogue was, or was not, present. It is also useful in determining what aspects of a given interaction may need to be changed.

Table 11.1 SKILLED DIALOGUE SELF-ASSESSMENT

RATING	Choosing Relationship over Control	Setting the Stage for Miracles
1 **Basic Awareness**	I understand and can define basic concepts associated with Skilled Dialogue (e.g., reciprocity, responsiveness, paradox, funds of knowledge, 3rd Space) YES NO SOMEWHAT	
2 **Beginning Applications**	_____ I can describe a range of diverse perspectives, behaviors, values, practices and belief systems (e.g., various child rearing practices) YES NO SOMEWHAT	_____I demonstrate ability to "stay with the tension" of contradictory perspectives without needing to defend or explain my own perspective or to resolve the tension in some other way YES NO SOMEWHAT
3 **Intermediate**	_____I acknowledge validity of diverse perspectives by accurately identifying their underlying meaning within a given context YES NO SOMEWHAT	_____I equalize power across interactions by identifying and exploring the value of another's diverse perspectives YES NO SOMEWHAT

Applications 4	_____I recognize others' contributions and resources in relation to specific interactions and situations YES NO SOMEWHAT	_____I can reframe contradictions into complementary perspectives independently and with fluency YES NO SOMEWHAT
5 Mastery	_____I consistently communicate respect, establish reciprocity and demonstrate responsiveness when interacting with others whose perspectives differ from my own; others report feeling accepted and valued when interacting with me YES NO SOMEWHAT	_____I consistently create responses that integrate others' diverse perspectives with my own in such a way as to access the strengths of those diverse perspectives YES NO SOMEWHAT

Table 11.2. Skilled Dialogue Guide To Dispositions and Qualities

	CHOOSING RELATIONSHIP OVER CONTROL	*SETTING THE STAGE*
RESPECT Honors identity **(ABOUT RECOGNIZING BOUNDARIES)**	<u>Key Guideline</u>: *Identify and relate to diverse ways in which experience is perceived & structured across diverse cultures/ perspectives.* <u>Key Question</u>: *Do my interactions reflect my understanding of the diverse ways in which others perceive & structure their world/experiences?* <u>Sample Strategies</u>: *-- listen mindfully; allow time between hearing others' words and interpreting meaning* *-- establish rapport* *-- get information about others' values, beliefs, worldview/ perspective*	<u>Key Guideline</u>: **Avoid polarization and stay with the tension of** *contradictory beliefs/values/ behaviors/perspectives.* <u>Key Question</u>: *Am I staying with the tension of contradictory beliefs, values, and behaviors "(i.e., culture bumps")?* <u>Sample Strategies</u>: *-- release natural inclination to fix/focus on solutions* *-- share verbal indicators of nonjudgmental attention (e.g., "I see," "That's interesting")* *-- acknowledge others' perspective w/o explaining or defending your own* *-- identify and reflect on specific culture bumps*

RECIPROCITY *Honors voice* **(ABOUT VALUING)**	Key Guideline: *Invite others to tell their "story" (i.e., describe their perspective).* Key Question*: Am I inviting other to "tell their story" (i.e., describe their perspective(s)?* Sample Strategies: -- *Trust that others' contributions are of equal value to mine* -- *Clarify your understanding of others' stories* -- *identify resources others bring to interaction* -- *identify "gift" of others diverse perspectives (i.e., what you can learn/receive from other)*	Key Guideline: *Recognize that there is always more than one perspective (i.e., enter "you're right and I'm right" paradox)* Key Question*: Am I appreciating the "rightness" or "gift" of others' perspectives ("story") in relation to my own?* Sample Strategies: -- *recognize that there is no need to make one perspective wrong in order to justify the other as right* -- *shift focus of conversation to balance participation* -- *give examples of how diverse ideas/behaviors can be integrated w/o changing (e.g., green + yellow= blue)*

	Key Guideline: *Present others' perspective(s) in such a way that other feels confident you find it meaningful and understand it as they do* Key Question: *How aware am I of what limits or obstructs my ability/ willingness to respond in meaningful ways to other?* Sample Strategies: *-- remain mindful and open to all that is unknown* *-- keep asking questions/ clarifying* *-- reflect understanding of others' perspective* *-- identify strengths of other's views re: current situation*	Key Guideline: *Integrate own perspective and other's perspective so as to generate a larger "whole" inclusive of both* Key Question: *Am I exploring how diverse perspectives are complementary with the intent to better perceive the greater more inclusive "frame" that unites them?* Sample Strategies: *-- reframe; tell stories differently; use different lenses* *-- integrate strengths of each perspective* *-- find common concern underlying differences*
RESPONSIVENESS *Honors connection* **(ABOUT BEING OPEN TO "NOT KNOWING")**		

Isaura Barrera, Ph.D. & Lucinda Kramer, Ph.D.

Table 11.3. Skilled Dialogue Analysis Sheet

I. Description of Interaction

Participants: Setting:

Purpose/Problem:

History:
(Was this a first meeting? Had there been previous meetings? Did you or other come to interactions with feelings/expectations based on previous interactions?)

II. Specific Analysis of Interaction(s)

CHOOSING RELATIONSHIP OVER CONTROL	SETTING THE STAGE FOR MIRACLES
Was I disposed to choose relationship over control? (i.e., did I use words and behaviors the acknowledged my acceptance of diverse boundaries as creative evidence-based expression of identity?) (low) 2 **3** (some) 4 **5** (high) What helped or hindered my willingness to adopt this disposition?	Was I disposed to Set the Stage for Miracles? (i.e., did I stay with the tension between what I wanted to see/hear and the other was saying/doing?) (low) 2 **3** (some) 4 **5** (high) What helped or hindered my willingness to adopt this disposition?

STRATEGIES

Welcoming (To what degree did I communicate that I welcomed the other as someone I could learn from?) (low)　2　**3** (some)　4　**5** (high) Behaviors/actions that supported or limited this strategy:	**Allow**ing (To what degree did I allow the other to express him/herself without interrupting or explaining/ defending my own views?) (low)　2　**3** (some)　4　**5** (high) Behaviors/actions that supported or limited this strategy:
Sense-Making (To what degree was I able to make sense of the other's views enough to understand them as valid and evidence-based within their context?) (low)　2　**3** (some)　4　**5** (high) Behaviors/actions that supported or limited this strategy:	**Appreciating** (To what degree was I able to appreciate the other's views as something of value that could make a postive contribution to our interaction?) (low)　2　**3** (some)　4　**5** (high) Behaviors/actions that supported or limited this strategy:
Joining (To what degree was I able to express the other's views in ways that the other felt were accurate and valid?) (low)　2　**3** (some)　4　**5** (high) Behaviors/actions that supported or limited this strategy:	**Harmonizing** (To what degree was I able to create 3rd Space; i.e., generate response options that were complementary and inclusive of both my perspective and the other's perspective?) (low)　2　**3** (some)　4　**5** (high) Behaviors/actions that supported or limited this strategy:

ADDITIONAL COMMENTS ON INTERACTION IF NECESSARY

III. Overall Evaluation of Interaction

Use of Skilled Dialogue:

(Limited/weak)   2   **3** (OK)   4   **5** (Strong)

Level of Satisfaction with Outcome(s):

(Low)   2   **3** (OK)   4   **5** (High)

COMMENTS:

References

Anderson, C. (2016). *TED talks: The official TED guide to public speaking.* NY: Houghton Mifflin Harcourt

Barrera, I, Corso, R.M. & MacPherson, D. (2003). *Skilled dialogue: Strategies for responding to cultural diversity in early childhood.* Baltimore: Paul Brookes.

Barrera, I. & Kramer, L. (2009). *Using Skilled Dialogue to transform challenging interactions.* Baltimore: Paul Brookes.

Bourgeault, C. (2015). *The holy trinity and the law of three: discovering the radical truth at the heart of Christianity.* Boston: Shambala

Bryner, A. & Markova, D. (1996). *An Unused Intelligence: Physical Thinking for the 21st Century.* Berkeley, CA: Conari Press.

Childs, C. (1998). *The spirit's terrain: Creativity, activism and transformation.* Boston: MA: Beacon Press.

Cloud, H. (2016). *The power of the other: The startling effect other people have on you, from the boardroom to the bedroom and beyond—and what to do about it.* NY: HarperCollins

Ellinor, L. & Gerard, G. (2014). *Dialogue: Rediscover the transforming power of conversation.* Hertford, NC: Crossroad Press

Fletcher, J.L & Olwyler, K. (1997). *Paradoxical Thinking: How to profit from your contradictions.* San Franisco, CA: Berrett-Koehler Publishers.

Gernsbacher, M. A. (2006). Toward a behavior of reciprocity. *Journal of Developmental Processes*, 139-152., I

Gladwell, M. *Choice, Happiness and Spaghetti Sauce*. TED Talk 9/2006

Goleman, D. (2006). *Social intelligence: The new science of human relationships*. NY: Bantam

Groome, T. (1980). *Christian religious education*. NY: Harper & Row

Iacoboni, M. (2009). Imitation, empathy, and mirror neurons. *Annual review of psychology*, 60: 653-70

Isaacs, W. (1999). *Dialogue and the art of thinking together*. NY: Doubleday

Jaworski, J. (2011). *Source: The inner path of knowledge creation*. San Francisco: Berrett-Koehler.

Jaworski, J. (1996). *Synchronicity: The inner path of leadership*. San Francisco: Berrett-Koehler.

Kahane, A. (2007). *Solving tough problems: An open way of talking, listening, and creating new realities*. San Francisco: Berrett-Koehler

Langer, E. J. (2005). *On becoming an artist*. New York: Ballantine Books

Lawrence-Lightfoot, S. (1999). *Respect*. Cambridge, MA: Perseus

Markova, D, & McArthur, A. (2015). *Collaborative intelligence: Thinking with people who think differently*. NY: Spiegel & Grau

Needleman, J. (2003). *A sense of the cosmos: Scientific knowledge and spiritual truth*. Rhinebeck, NY: Monkfish Book Publishing.

Newberg, A., D'Aquili, E. & Krause, V. (2001). *Why God won't go away*. NY: Ballantine.

Markus, H. R. & Kitayama, S. (2003). Models of agency: Sociocultural diversity in the construction of action. In V. Murphy-Berman & J. J. Berman (Eds.). *Cross-cultural perspectives of the self: Nebraska Symposium on Motivation*, v. 49 (p. 2-57). Lincoln University of Nebraska Press.

Palmer, P. (1997). *The courage to teach.* San Francisco, CA: Jossey-Bass.

Perkins, D. (2000). *The eureka effect: The art and logic of breakthrough thinking.* NY: W.W. Norton.

Remen, R. N. (2000). *My grandfather's blessings.* NY: Riverhead Books

Rizzolatte, G., Fogassi, I. & Gallese, V. (2006, November). Mirrors in the mind, *Scientific American*, 295(5), 54-61.

Rosinski, P. (2003). *Coaching across cultures: New tools for leveraging national, corporate, and professional differences.* Yarmouth, ME: Nicholas Brealey.

Seelig, T. (2012). *InGenius: A crash course on creativity.* NY: Harper One.

Senge, P.M., Scharmer, C.O., Jaworski, J. & Flowers, B.S. (2004). *Presence: Human purpose and the field of the future.* Cambridge, MA: Society for Organizational Learning.

Shapiro, D. (2017). *Negotiating the nonnegotiable: How to resolve your most emotionally charged conflicts.* NY: Viking.

Stone, D, Patton, B. & Heen, S.(1999). *Difficult conversations.* New York: Viking Adult.

Wheatley, M. J. (2005). *Finding our way: Leadership for an uncertain time.* San Francisco: Berrett-Koehler.

Yaconelli, M. (1998). *Dangerous wonder: The adventure of childlike faith.* Grand Rapids: MI: Zondervan Publishing Company.

Zaiss, C. (2002). *True partnership: Revolutionary thinking about relating to others.* San Francisco: Berrett-Koehler.

www.bloomberg.com, 9/10/15, *Take a virtual walk through a Syrian refugee camp.*

www.changingminds.org, Changing minds and persuasion—How we change what others think

www.thework.com, The work of Byron Katie.

Endnotes

1   www.Huffingpost.com This article is well-worth reading in its entirety not just in relation to university speakers but also and perhaps more importantly in relation to its implications for collaboration and communication across diverse perspectives in all situations

2   Examples abound in the political arena and other arenas where highly charged issues are at stake. Even, we have found, in hypothetical roleplays!

3   The scope of this book prohibits a comprehensive explanation of these aspects; readers are referred to the referenced work for more detailed information

4   More information on the early identification of these perceptions and the two people who served as original models can be found in Barrera, I., Corso, R., & Macpherson, D. (2003). *Skilled Dialogue: Strategies for responding to cultural diversity in early childhood.* Baltimore, MD: Paul H. Brookes Publishing.

5   It is interesting or perhaps more accurately ironic that it is the same people whom we wish to acquire new learning as we communicate and collaborate with them that we so often judge as somehow unable to learn the "right" behavior as we have!

6   There are master practitioners in both the fields of mental health and education who honor their clients'/students' identities and can establish reciprocal relationships in which they are open to learning as well as to teaching even when they also need to contain or report harmful behaviors. Unfortunately, neither the scope of this book nor our own expertise permits discussion of Skilled Dialogue in relation to these contexts.

7   This observation is a central premise in Markova, D, & McArthur, A. (2015). *Collaborative intelligence: Thinking with people who think differently.* NY: Spiegel & Grau, which is an invaluable resource for understanding how differences enrich rather than detract or divide.

8   For purposes of clarity it needs to be noted that 3rd Space should not be confused with the term *Third Space* or with other similar terms found in a wide range of literature.

9   In contrast to Michigan, where the leader was from, rain in South Texas, where the institute was taking place, is commonly triggered as a result of a

cool and dry weather front from the north that pushes out warm and humid air from the Gulf of Mexico.

[10] See endnote #6 and related material

[11] www.bloomberg.com, 9/10/15, Take a virtual walk through a Syrian refugee camp This report has links to actual excerpts of the material to which it refers.

[12] These strategies, like all Skilled Dialogue strategies, were distilled from observations of skilled communicators and collaborators. Readers are referred to the authors' earlier books for more information.

[13] It is difficult to share this incident. I do so, however, to emphasize the importance of honoring someone's identity as who they are not as who they seem or who we think they are

[14] Byron Katie's work addresses asking the question "Is it true?" for much the same purpose (www.thework.com)

[15] In over 20 years of practicing Skilled Dialogue, we have yet to fail find a thread of commonality between diverse perspectives, beliefs, and/or behaviors, even then these appeared totally contradictory.

[16] Graphic designs by Joseph Kethan, One on One Tech Ed Services, San Antonio, TX. Thanks, Joe

Printed in the United States
By Bookmasters